# STANDARD GRADE HISTORY
# Scotland and Britain

since 1830

## THIRD EDITION

## Sandra Chalmers and Larry Cheyne

### Series Editor: Graeme Coy

**Cover Photograph:** the cover photograph shows George Wyllie's *The Straw Locomotive* which hung from the Finnieston Crane for several months in 1998. The crane is a remaining testimony to Glasgow's – and Scotland's – industrial and trading heritage. The locomotive also symbolised this heritage, and the contribution made to Scotland's wealth by the Railway Age. The locomotive was eventually lowered, transported to Springburn (previously the site of Europe's largest railway engineering works) and was then burned, to reveal a large question mark at the heart of the locomotive…

## Hodder Gibson
A MEMBER OF THE HODDER HEADLINE GROUP

# Acknowledgements

The publishers would like to thank the following individuals, institutions and companies for permission to reproduce photographs in this book: Aberdeen City Arts (page 58), Aberdeen University Library (page 17), Austin Rover (page 55), Batsford Publications (page 62), Beamish Museum (page 43 top), Caledonian Railway Association (page 19 top), City of Aberdeen Technical Services (page 46), Corbis (pages 35, 47, 50, 53 bottom, 61, 88 top, 89 both, 93), Doug Lean (page 13), Equal Opportunities Commission (page 83), Express Newspapers (page 96), '50 special years' by Tom Begg (page 71), George Washington Wilson Photographic Archive (pages 21, 53 top), Glasgow Herald (pages 80, 82, 94), Great North of Scotland Railway Association (page 53 right), Hodder and Stoughton (pages 4, 14, 23, 41 top, 57), Hulton Archives (pages 11, 44, 48, 56 all, 107 both), Ian Jolly/Northpix (page 104), Imperial War museum (page 67), Keystone Press Agency (page 110), Mary Evans Picture Library (pages 6, 8, 23 left, 30, 31, 49, 105), The Mitchell Library/Graham Collection (page 60), Museum of London (page 66 both), National Motor Museum (page 88 middle and bottom), NMSI (pages 9, 19 bottom, 52 both), Punch (pages 27), Science Photo Library (pages 97, 98), Topham Picturepoint (pages 41 bottom, 42, 43 bottom).

The publishers would also like to thank the following for permission to reproduce material in this book:

Extracts from **All Our Working Lives by Peter Pagnamenta & Richard Overy** reproduced with the permission of BBC Worldwide Limited. Copyright © Peter Pagnamenta & Richard Overy 1984. Pearson Education Limited for extracts from **English Social History** by G. M. Trevelyan and **Keir Hardie and the Rise of the Labour Party** by Hyman Shapiro.

Orders: please contact Bookpoint Ltd, 130 Milton Park, Abingdon, Oxon OX14 4SB. Telephone: (44) 01235 827720. Fax: (44) 01235 400454. Lines are open from 9.00 – 6.00, Monday to Saturday, with a 24 hour message answering service. You can also order through our website www.hoddereducation.co.uk. Hodder Gibson can be contacted direct on: Tel: 0141 848 1609; Fax: 0141 889 6315; email: hoddergibson@hodder.co.uk

*British Library Cataloguing in Publication Data*
A catalogue record for this title is available from the British Library

ISBN-10: 0 340 81437 3
ISBN-13: 978 0 340 81437 6

First Edition Published 1998
Second Edition Published 2000
This Edition Published 2004
Impression number   10 9 8 7 6 5 4 3 2
Year                      2007  2006

Cover photo from the Glasgow Digital Library
Typeset by Fakenham Photosetting Ltd, Fakenham, Norfolk.
Printed in Italy for Hodder Gibson, 2A Christie Street, Paisley, PA1 1NB.

# Contents

# Preface

The chapters in this new version in the Standard Grade History series have undergone further revisions to extend and amend text, sources and activities in line with the needs of students and the demands of the Standard Grade Examinations since 1999.

As in earlier versions, the revised books contain a blend of narrative and source evidence, written and visual. Chapters are still presented in two parts, the first designed for those working towards success at Foundation/General levels and the second supporting those aiming at General/Credit levels.

The Activities which follow each section are related to the information and evidence in the section and to the Knowledge and Enquiry criteria on which the Standard Grade examination is based. Activities are coded to highlight the criteria to which they relate.

In addition, a new introductory chapter and a glossary have been added to the books. Also there is an annotated list of internet resources.

*Graeme Coy 2003*

# Introduction: studying history and passing exams

## History is a Mystery – and solving it can be great fun!

Learning about the past involves detective work. In order to know and understand events from years gone by, how people lived, what they thought and did, you have to try to solve a whole series of puzzles – some much more complicated than others.

To find out about history, especially the recent past, you probably started by asking parents, grandparents, and teachers. For most of the more distant past you have to use a wider variety of evidence to build a picture you can see and understand. Part of the detective work involves finding relevant sources of evidence and then trying to fit these together to make as clear and accurate a picture as you can.

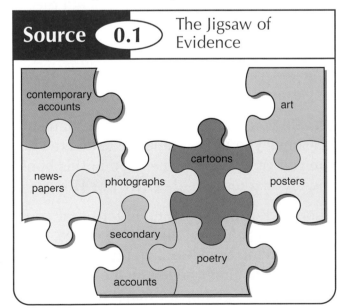

**Source** **0.1** The Jigsaw of Evidence

contemporary accounts

art

cartoons

news-papers

photographs

posters

secondary

poetry

accounts

Each of the pieces in the jigsaw is valuable but as you can see the jigsaw is not complete. This is a problem which faces all historians! Usually you have to try to see the past using only some of the evidence you might like to have. In this book you will find many types of historical evidence, such as:

◆ written personal accounts,

◆ official records,

◆ quotations from other history books,

◆ newspaper and magazine extracts,

◆ letters, poetry, memoirs,

◆ pictures, cartoons, photographs, maps.

You can use these to help you reconstruct and understand the past, but there is other evidence which cannot go into a book, such as films, artefacts (clothes, tools, weapons) and archaeological evidence. The more evidence you can use and the more skilfully you can use it, the better and more accurate will be your picture of the past!

## Using Evidence and Passing Examinations

There are several different things you can do with historical evidence. You can use it to gain KNOWLEDGE and UNDERSTANDING [KU] or to make an ENQUIRY. [ENQ]

◆ You can use evidence to describe something, such as why a war started, what someone did, how important an invention was. [KU]

◆ You can use it to decide what the person or persons who produced it thought or wanted others to think.[ENQ]

◆ You can compare pieces of evidence to see if they agree or disagree or to help you reach your own conclusions.[ENQ]

◆ You can make up your own mind about the value of evidence, based on such things as WHEN it was produced, WHY it was produced, HOW it was produced and WHO produced it.[ENQ].

Not many people like sitting Examinations. Yet an examination, especially one set and marked by people who do not know you, is a very good way for you to prove what you can do. Most people train and prepare better when they know there is a game or race or test at the end! Books like this help your training by building your knowledge and skills and confidence. Here are some suggestions to help you succeed.

◆ Remember the examination is meant to give you an opportunity to show what you can do. It is NOT full of traps and tricks to find out what you cannot do. Both you and the examiners know what topics you have been studying and the examination will be based on some of these. Sources will be like ones you have used – they may even be the same in some cases!

◆ When you sit an examination look carefully for the contexts you have studied and answer ONLY those ones.

◆ Read sources and questions carefully to decide what it is you are asked to do. AND look at he number of marks for each question to help you decide how much to write in your answer, so that you do not waste time writing too much.

◆ Never copy a whole source almost word for word into an answer, because this does not show that you understand or can use the source.

Questions like the following are asking you to show your **Knowledge and Understanding [KU]** of the past.

◆ What changes happened in Skye around 1840?

◆ Describe some of the dangers workers faced in coalmines in the 1840s.

◆ Why did war break out in Europe in 1914?

◆ How important was militarism to Nazi rule in Germany?

You are expected to use your **Enquiry [ENQ]** skills when you see the following,

◆ How useful is the source in explaining why changes happened in Skye around 1840?

◆ Do the sources agree about the dangers workers faced in coalmines in the 1840s?

◆ How fully does the source explain the outbreak of war in 1914?

◆ Does the author of the source think militarism was important to Nazi rule in Germany?

To help you, more of the different kinds of questions you have to answer and activities you can carry out are included in this book and are marked as either [KU] or [ENQ].

Good luck with any examinations that you sit. But if you follow the advice above, and use this book thoughtfully and carefully, then you shouldn't need any luck – and you should enjoy solving the many mysteries of history . . .

# Section A 1830–80

# 1 Scotland and Britain in 1830

## Society in 1830

Britain in 1830 was a very different country from today. The population was much smaller and you were very clearly separated into different classes according to:

◆ who your parents were;

◆ how rich they were;

◆ what job they did.

Look at Source 1.1 below to find out more about who belonged to which class and why. People from the different classes did not mix together much and it was not easy to move from one class to a higher one. Members of the aristocracy and the big landowners looked down on ordinary people and even on the rich merchants and businessmen who were helping to make Britain very wealthy.

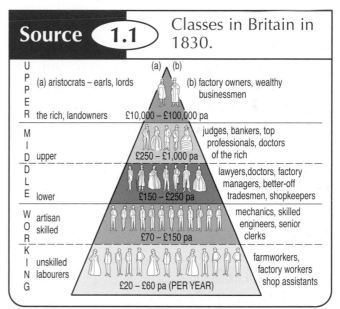

**Source 1.1** Classes in Britain in 1830.

UPPER
(a) aristocrats – earls, lords
the rich, landowners £10,000 – £100,000 pa
(b) factory owners, wealthy businessmen

MIDDLE
upper £250 – £1,000 pa
judges, bankers, top professionals, doctors of the rich

lower £150 – £250 pa
lawyers, doctors, factory managers, better-off tradesmen, shopkeepers

WORKING
artisan skilled £70 – £150 pa
mechanics, skilled engineers, senior clerks

unskilled labourers £20 – £60 pa (PER YEAR)
farmworkers, factory workers, shop assistants

## Growing population

In 1830 the number of people in Britain was increasing rapidly. Source 1.2 shows the increase between 1811 and 1891. The table comes from information collected by the Government in a census (counting) of all the people in Britain.

**Source 1.2** Census figures.

| Year | Scotland | Great Britain |
|------|----------|---------------|
| 1811 | 1.8 million | 11.9 million |
| 1831 | 2.3 million | 16.2 million |
| 1851 | 2.9 million | 20.8 million |
| 1871 | 3.3 million | 26.0 million |
| 1891 | 4.0 million | 33.0 million |

**F/G LEVEL**

This great rise in population was caused by people having larger families (rising birth rate), living longer (falling death rate) and more people coming to live in Britain (immigrating) than were leaving it (emigrating).

In 1801 only one-quarter of British people lived in towns but more and more were moving there in search of work. By 1851 over half lived in towns and the number increased to almost three-quarters by the end of the nineteenth century.

## Activities

1 Draw a pyramid like that in Source 1.1 and place the five people below in their correct place in society:

     judge
     engineer
     factory owner
     factory worker
     lord **(KU)**

2 Write a sentence or two about each of the people saying:

   a) what class they belong to

   b) who is rich and who is poor

   c) who looks up to whom. **(KU)**

3 Explain why many people in Britain were not happy about the way members of the top class treated those in the lower classes. **(KU)**

4 Explain why the population of Scotland (and Britain) rose in the nineteenth century? **(KU)**

**CREDIT LEVEL**

# Migration

People moved to the towns for a variety of reasons. In Scotland some came from the Lowland countryside.

Many others came to towns like Glasgow from the Highlands and Islands where the land was poor and landlords had discovered they could make much greater profits from sheep. In Sutherland there were around 15 000 sheep in 1811 but by 1855 there were 204 000. To make way for the sheep, the landlords evicted the tenants who lived there. This is called the **Highland Clearances**.

These clearances caused ill-feeling because entire villages were forced to go to the coast, the Lowlands or places like Canada and America.

**Source**   **1.3**   This is a description of people in Glasgow in 1838, written by one of them.

*Taking Glasgow as the centre, there are persons who have come to it from ... around 60 miles. My father originally came from the Lothians, and had been a country farmer. He was driven out by the improvements in farming, became a mechanic, and settled in Glasgow. ... When the small farms disappeared and the cottagers were driven from their agricultural employments, they first collected in villages, and then gradually moved to the large towns.*

It was not only because of evictions that the population of the Highlands fell. Look at Source 1.4 from 'The Scotsman' newspaper. In the late 1840s the prices of Highland cattle fell at the market in Falkirk.

> **Source 1.4** From 'The Scotsman' newspaper of 15 August 1849.
>
> *Not a worse market for 20 years. It is not possible to get the small Highland beasts sold at any price.*

Unfortunately, this was also the time potato crops were hit by a disease called the blight. These conditions made many destitute and forced them to leave farming.

**Source 1.5** Examples of crop failure in 1849.

| District | Description of Crop Failure |
|---|---|
| Wester Ross | two-thirds of crop |
| Mull | near complete failure |
| West Highlands | loss estimated at one-quarter to one-half |

Between 1851 and 1891 the population of the rural Highlands dropped by almost one tenth – the same amount as in rural counties in the Lowlands. In 1883 the Government set up the Napier Commission to look into the conditions of the Highlanders. Three years later the Crofters' Holding Act of 1886 gave the crofters the 'three Fs':

◆ fair rents decided by an independent group

◆ fixed tenure (they could not be evicted as long as they paid their rents)

◆ freedom of a son to inherit his father's land.

These changes did not stop the movement of people from the Highlands and the population of the crofting areas dropped from 180 000 in 1881 to 120 000 in 1931. Many left to find an easier way of life and higher wages.

From the early nineteenth century, people came from Ireland to do seasonal work on the land or to help build railways. Many eventually immigrated permanently, particularly to the Glasgow area, as Source 1.6 describes.

> **Source 1.6** The historian J. E. Handley described the movement of the population in 'The Irish in Scotland', published in 1947.
>
> *The coal, iron and textile industries (of Lanarkshire) attracted tens of thousands of immigrants in search of work. ... With this expansion of Glasgow came the growth of the Irish population. ... The decline of the linen and woollen industries in the north of Ireland and the rise of the cotton industry in the west of Scotland attracted Irish towards the city.*

By 1840 it was reckoned that one person in four living in Glasgow was Irish. The number increased in the 1840s when potato blight in Ireland caused great hardship there and 1.5 million people died. Many others came to Scotland to escape starvation.

3

**Source** 1.7

This was drawn in the 1840s by an artist who visited Ireland and shows how problems there were shown in the British Press.

## Activities

1  Explain why it would be almost impossible for an engineer to be accepted as an equal by a lord in the nineteenth century. **(KU)**

2  Use sources 1.3, 1.4 and 1.5 to explain why many Scots came to live in and around Glasgow. **(KU)**

3  Use sources 1.6 and 1.7 to explain why the Irish

a)  left their own country

b)  came to the west of Scotland. **(KU)**

4  Is source 1.7 useful evidence about the growing popultion in towns in Britain during the 1840s? **(ENQ)**

# 2 People at work: Agriculture

The Census of 1831 showed that farming was still the most common way of earning a living. In England, over one million families worked on the land. The food they produced fed most of the population. In Scotland also, agriculture was the most important industry in the country. Two-thirds of the population worked for farmers for wages, which were often low. Labourers in the South of England earned as little as 7 shillings (35p) a week.

Hours of work were often long, and the work hard. This was true for men, working as skilled ploughmen or as labourers, and for women, both outdoors as dairy maids and indoors as farm servants.

**Source 2.1** In 1833 William Cobbett MP described the life of farm workers in 'A Tour of Scotland'.

*Six days, from daylight to dark, these good and laborious people work. A married man receives in money about four pounds for the year. He also gets oats, barley, peas and potatoes. He pays for his own fuel; he must find a woman to reap for twenty whole days in the harvest, as payment for the rent of his bothie. They never have wheat bread, nor beef nor mutton, though the land is covered with wheat and cattle.*

*The farm yards are, in fact, factories for making corn and meat, carried on mainly by means of horses and machinery.*

Farming was changing. More and more open fields were being enclosed. Farmers were becoming more willing to try new methods. New steam-powered machinery was appearing.

**Source 2.2** A description of farming from 1855.

*Nearly every farm in the Lothians has its steam engine. In the county of Haddington, which contains about 200 000 acres, there were, in 1853, 185 steam engines.*

One result of the use of machinery was to cut the number of jobs on the land. Wages stayed low, or even fell. More and more men left the land to look for jobs in the cities. Even the city slums seemed better than working 12 or 14 hours a day, in all weathers, to live in a hut with no water or toilet, on a diet in which meat, or even cheese, was a little known luxury.

**Source 2.4** **Harry Snell**, a former farm worker, remembered farm work:

*Farm work was exhausting, looked down on, and grossly underpaid. It was dangerous; you were out in all weathers. Very few of those who managed to escape it returned of their own free will.*

**Source** 2.3 An example of a steam threshing machine.

## Activities

**1** Was farm work well paid? Give evidence to support your answer. **(KU)**

**2** Why is Cobbett's 'A Tour of Scotland' a good source of evidence about life on the land at this time? **(ENQ)**

**3** What shows that farming was a very important industry in Britain in the 1830s? **(KU)**

**4** What complaints did farm workers have at this time about:
   their hours of work
   the work they did
   the homes they lived in? **(KU)**

## Changes in agriculture 1830–1880

Some historians have claimed that British farming did very well indeed in the middle years of the nineteenth century. They call the period a 'Golden Age' for agriculture because many farmers enjoyed high prices for their produce and could pay their rents easily. Farmers were encourged to produce more and were willing to try more and more new methods. Look back at Source 2.2 for evidence of this and also at Source 2.5.

## Free trade and the repeal of the corn laws

In the 1840s, the Government changed its attitude to trade between Britain and other countries. This new approach was known as 'Free Trade'. With Free Trade, goods could come into Britain without paying tariffs – duty free. This made goods much cheaper to buy. Farmers wanted tariffs on foreign corn to stay and the Conservative Government, led by Robert Peel and supported by Tory landowners, agreed. In 1845, however, a terrible famine broke out in Ireland. Fearing a million deaths, Peel abandoned the Corn Laws.

## Source 2.5 — New methods of production.

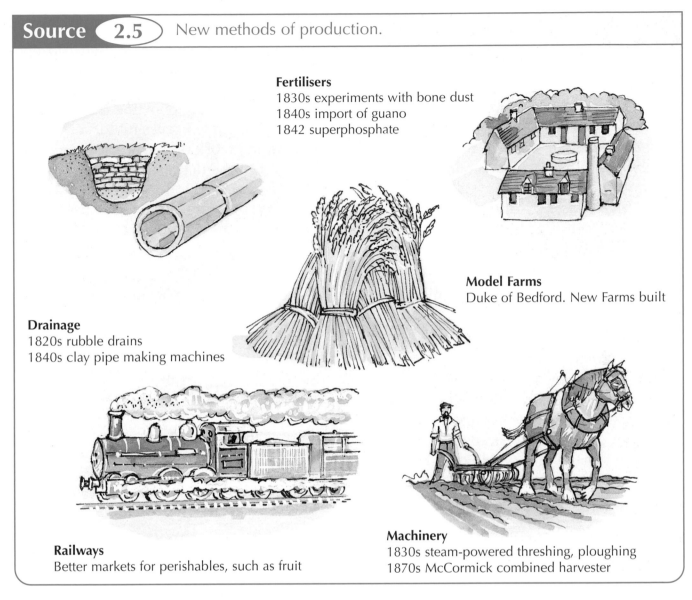

**Fertilisers**
1830s experiments with bone dust
1840s import of guano
1842 superphosphate

**Model Farms**
Duke of Bedford. New Farms built

**Drainage**
1820s rubble drains
1840s clay pipe making machines

**Railways**
Better markets for perishables, such as fruit

**Machinery**
1830s steam-powered threshing, ploughing
1870s McCormick combined harvester

British farmers were hardly affected by their repeal. The next 25 years were more prosperous than ever. But in Ireland, 1 500 000 people starved, and many more were forced to emigrate. For them, the repeal of the Corn Laws came too late.

## Changes in rural life

The most obvious change in the countryside was migration. Better diet and less disease lead to an increase in the number of people living in the countryside. At the same time the changes in farming meant there were fewer jobs for farm labourers. The 1851 Census showed that about 2 000 000 people in Britain worked in agriculture; only 20 years later the Census showed that the figure was down to 1 700 000. Put another way, one male in six (aged 10 or above) was a farm labourer; by 1881 it was only one in ten.

Wages for farm work varied from time to time and from place to place. They were higher when harvests were good and there was a lot of work or when there were jobs in mining or other industries nearby to tempt farm workers away from the land. This happened in the North of England and Central Scotland. Here, wages for a skilled

7

CREDIT LEVEL

ploughman could be as high as £50 per year during the good years of the 1860s, but could drop to £30 per year in bad times.

Women's wages were usually half those of men. In places like Dorset in the South of England wages for men were about £14 per year, while in the Highlands and Islands of Scotland wages were lower still. In some places there was a 'Hiring Fair' once or twice each year at which men and women bargained with farmes for jobs as ploughmen or labourers or as kitchen workers. Each worker had to try to make the best deal he or she could.

In Scotland, where most workers lived on the farm, employers sometimes promised workers warm, dry housing and good food but what they actually gave them was space in a draughty loft above a barn or workshop or in a cold, damp bothy, living on oatmeal made into porridge or brose.

## Farm labourers' union

In the Midlands of England in 1872, Joseph Arch founded the Agricultural Labourers' Union. By the end of the year it had 100 000 members, supporting the union's aims which included pressing for a minimum wage of 80p per week for a 9.5 hour day. But the depression in agriculture after 1873 meant that farm workers threatening to strike could easily be replaced, and the union collapsed.

## New machines

New machinery and tools also weakened the farm workers' position. Even replacing the old sickle with the long-bladed two-handed scythe meant workers could cut twice as much hay or wheat. Bell's reaper, introduced widely by 1850, meant that one man, with two horses, could do the work of a dozen men.

**Source** 2.6 Threshing of grain using new farming machinery.

Likewise, a steam threshing machine could, in a day, prepare as much grain – threshed, cleaned, and ready for sale – as a dozen men, using flails, could in a month! This was disastrous news for labourers who depended on work like threshing to see them through the winter, when other work was scarce.

| Source | 2.7 | Bell's reaping machine |
|---|---|---|

| Source | 2.8 | In 1944, G. M. Trevelyan wrote 'English Social History' in which he pointed out: |
|---|---|---|

*The lady, then the farmers' wives, and lastly the labourers' wives, learnt to buy in the town many articles that used to be made in the village. One by one the craftsmen disappeared – the harness-maker, the miller, the weaver – till by the end of the century the village blacksmith was the only craftsman left.*

Even the growth of industries and the improvements in roads and railways had a down side.

CREDIT LEVEL

## Activities

1  Do you think Peel was right to repeal the Corn Laws? **(KU)**

2  Was the period 1830 to 1870 'the golden age of British agriculture'? Consider reasons for and against in your answer. **(KU)**

3  Explain why farm workers found it so difficult to get reasonable wages. **(KU)**

4  How important were new machines to the (lives of) farm workers? **(KU)**

# 3 People at work: Industry

## Coal mines in the nineteenth century

During the nineteenth century yearly output of coal rose rapidly

1830    30 million tons a year
1880   150 million tons a year.

Likewise, the number of people employed in mining rose from 219 000 in 1851 to 503 900 in 1881, by which time only agriculture employed more people.

In the 1830s, working conditions in the mines were not good. After the Factory Act of 1833 was passed, Lord Shaftesbury got Parliament to set up an enquiry into conditions in the mines. In 1842 the Children's Employment Commission published its Report on the Collieries and Iron-works in the East of Scotland. The Commissioners talked to people working in the mines and included what they had to say in the Report.

**Source 3.1** Three extracts from the 1842 Children's Employment Commission report.

*a) Janet Cumming, 11 years old.*

*I work with my father and have done so for two years. Father starts at two in the morning; I start with the women at five and come up at five at night. I work all night on Fridays, and come up at twelve on Saturday.*

*I carry coal from the face to the pit-bottom. The weight is usually a hundredweight, and the distance between 50 and 80 yards. The roof is very low; I have to bend my back and legs, and the water often comes up to the calves of my legs. I have no liking for the work, but father makes me like it.*

*b) George Reid, 16 years old.*

*I pick coal at the coal face. I have done this for six years. The seam is 26 inches high and when I pick I have to twist myself up. It is horrible sore work; none ever come up for meals. Pieces of bread are taken down. Six of the family work with father below; when work is good he takes away £1 to £1.25 a week.*

*c) Jane Watson, age 40.*

*I have worked underground for 33 years. I have had nine children and two dead born, which was due to the work. I have always had to work till the birth, and return after 10 or 12 days.*

*It is only horse-work, and ruins the women; it makes them old at 40. Women get so weak that they are forced to take the little ones down to help them, even children of six years old.*

The Commission also published drawings of conditions underground, like this.

| Source 3.2 | Working in the coal mines. |

## Activities

Imagine you worked in a coal mine in 1842.

1 Choose a job underground.

 Give your evidence to the Commission about your work.

 Mention
 ◆ the work you did
 ◆ the hours you worked
 ◆ the conditions you worked in
 ◆ whether or not you liked the work (give your reasons). **(KU)**

2 Say whether or not you thought the 1842 Mines Act was an important law. (Again, give your reasons.) **(KU)**

3 What dangers did miners face when they worked underground? **(KU)**

4 Compare the evidence given to the parliamentary enquiry into conditions in mines by Janet Cumming and George Reid. **(ENQ)**

5 Can you find other examples of drawings such as that showing conditions underground? **(ENQ)**

Coal was cut by men called 'hewers', like George Reid, who earned the highest wages. Often whole families worked down the mine. Older women were 'bearers' who carried heavy baskets of coal up ladders from the bottom of the mine shaft to the surface – sometimes they fell or dropped coal from their baskets. Older children, like Janet Cummings, carried coal from the hewers to the bottom of the mine shaft and younger children were 'trappers' who opened and closed the ventilation doors underground.

As a result of the evidence to the Commission, a Mines Act was passed in 1842. This said

◆ no women should work underground;

◆ no children under 10 should work underground;

◆ inspectors were appointed to make sure the rules were obeyed.

Many families faced hard times as a result of the Mines Act, because they could not find other work. Some tried to go on working underground but mine owners eventually stopped them. New inventions helped make work underground safer, like steel pit props to hold up the tunnels and steam power to lift coal to the surface.

The old dangers to mine workers still continued to kill thousands underground every year – explosions, poisonous gases, sudden floods.

# Changes in mining 1830–1880

## The demand for coal

Several industries needed increasing amounts of coal in this period.

◆ cotton manufacture used more and more steam powered machines;

◆ iron production used 4 tons of coal to make 1 ton of pure iron;

◆ more and more railways and steam powered ships appeared.

To meet these demands coal mines went deeper and larger. Look at Source 3.3 to see changes in mines beween 1830 and 1880. Mining, however, remained poorly-paid and dangerous. While miners were being paid between 12p and 25p a day – and women half that – the Duke of Hamilton drew royalties of £100 000 a year from the coal dug from beneath 'his' earth.

**Source** **3.3** Changes in coal mining between 1830 and 1880.

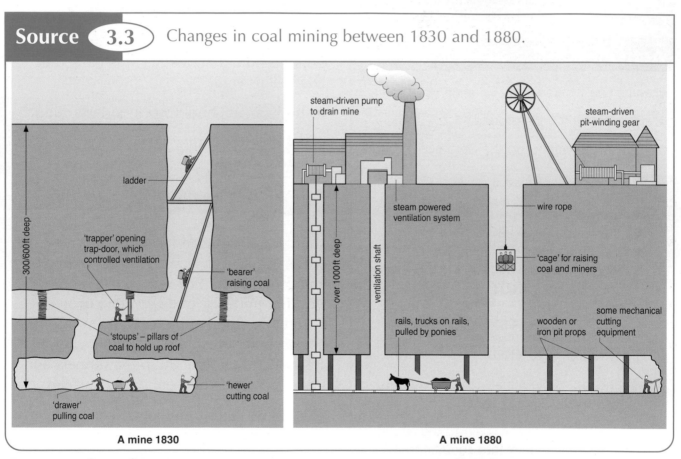

A mine 1830

A mine 1880

## Dangers in mines

Accidents were sadly all too frequent. Every five hours a miner was killed and every two minutes one was injured. Miners faced many dangers.

◆ There were gases, some were poisonous while others exploded with the tiniest spark;

◆ Floods happened when miners broke through into underground lakes;

◆ Cave-ins were the biggest threat and happened when the earth moved or not enough roof supports were left in place;

◆ Miners lost fingers, toes, eyes because of flying pieces of coal or stone;

◆ There was always coal dust filling the lungs of miners, a silent killer which brought on the 'black spit' and ruined miners lungs.

**Source 3.4** Working in a Black Country pit.

For women bearers, especially before 1842, carrying coal to the surface up long and unsafe ladders was very dangerous. Falls were common and coal or tools fell from the heavy baskets the bearers carried. Even where horses were used to pull coal or miners to the surface accidents were common because the boys who looked after them lost their concentration.

## Improvement in mines

Between 1830 and 1880, some improvements in safety did take place. Some were the result of Government action, such as better supervision of pit winding gear, responsible for lowering and raising miners. Pit managers had to have a certificate to show they were competent. Finally, single shaft pits were outlawed, so that if one shaft became blocked, miners could escape by another.

Other improvements were the result of technological changes, especially the wider use of steam power to raise coal and men, and to drive ventilation fans. Not all technological improvements had the desired effect. Accidents actually rose after Sir Humphrey Davy invented the miners' safety lamp; but this was largely due to the working of deeper and more dangerous seams that the lamp made possible.

## Activities

1   Why did output of coal grow so rapidly in this period? **(KU)**

2   Describe three dangers faced by those who worked in the mines in the late nineteenth century. **(KU)**

3   Were there important changes to working conditions in the mines between 1830 and 1880? **(KU)**

CREDIT LEVEL

# Railways 1830–1880

## Building the railways

In 1825, a group of Manchester factory owners raised £400 000 to build a railway between Liverpool and Manchester. They claimed it would cut the cost of transport by at least one-third. After the railway opened in 1830, they found the following facts:

**Source 3.5** An extract from the Annual Register, 1832.

*Coaches could only carry 688 persons per day; the railway carried an average of 1070 per day. The coach fare was 50p inside and 25p outside; by railway it is 25p inside and 17½p outside. The time by coach was four hours; by railway it is one hour and three quarters. Goods are delivered in Manchester the same day from Liverpool. By canal they were never delivered before the third day.*

The clear advantages of railways made other groups hurry to raise money to build railways. Gangs of labourers known as 'navvies' were hired to do the hard manual work of building them, as the following sources show.

**Source 3.6** Digging Bishopton cutting, near Renfrew, 1842.

Writing in 1851 J. R. Francis also described the lifestyle of the navvies:

**Source 3.7**

*They earned high wages, and spent them. Many of them lived in a drunken state until their money was spent, and they were forced to look for work again. They made their houses where they got their work. Some slept in huts of damp turf, too low to stand up in; the roof was small sticks, covered with straw. It mattered not to them that the rain beat through the roof, and that winds swept through the holes.*

One of the contractors called Peto, who employed navvies, described them to a Royal Commission in 1845 as follows:

**Source** 3.8 | Adapted from evidence to Royal Commission, 1845.

*I know navvies well. I find that if you pay them well and give them decent lodging, they are the most faithful creatures on earth. But if you pay them 2p a day and feed them on nothing but potatoes, can you wonder if they drink too much and cause trouble?*

The work was hard and dangerous. Using a pick and shovel, and sometimes gunpowder, each man shifted 20 tons of earth a day. Tunnelling was especially dangerous, with explosions and cave-ins claiming the lives of many.

**Source** 3.9 | Explosion of tunnel

UN COUP DE GRISOU

Navvies faced many other dangers too, as the following source describes.

**Source** 3.10 | I. Olson described the dangers in 'The Day the Railways Came to Strichen,' Leopard, 1994.

*Accidents were common. Men were trapped between wagons, became buried under falls of earth, with limbs broken and bodies crushed. Most recovered, some were disabled for life, but their workmates had a 'whip-round' to tide them over.*

## Activities

1 What four advantages did railways have over canals, according to the Annual Register? **(KU)**

2 Look at Source 3.8. How can you tell that Peto thought navvies were not all bad? **(KU)**

3 Why was the work of the navvies dangerous? **(KU)**

4 In what ways do Francis and Peto disagree about the navvies? (Use Sources 3.7 and 3.8). **(KU)**

FOUNDATION/GENERAL LEVEL

15

# The growth of the railway system

One problem faced by the railway companies was buying the land they needed from its owners.

**Source 3.11**

In 1838 this article appeared in Chambers' 'Edinburgh Review'.

*Scarcely any instance is known of a reasonable price being asked for the land wanted by the railway proprietors. One spirit pervades all – a determination to extort as much as they can. In dealing with railways, men think themselves entitled to cheat without restraint.*

Railways also faced opposition from those who feared that the coming of the railway would destroy scenery with embankments and cuttings, set farmland afire with sparks from the locomotive, disturb livestock and bring in undesirables from town and city. Others feared the coming of the navvies.

**Source 3.12**

An extract from 'The Day the Railways Came to Strichen' by I. Olson.

*There was an increase in assaults, thefts both small and serious, and public drunkenness – women as well as men. The Saturday navvy sprees were the worst; churchgoers on Sunday mornings had to avoid continuing street fights as they picked their way through drunken bodies littering the street.*

The local landowner in Strathpeffer was able to prevent the railway coming there for 30 years.

Despite this, the Scottish Railway system expanded, as shown in Source 3.13.

**Source 3.13** The Expansion of Scottish Railways, 1840–1880.

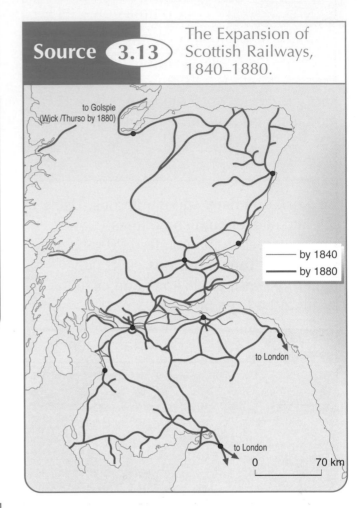

to Golspie (Wick /Thurso by 1880)

— by 1840
— by 1880

to London

to London

0        70 km

A similar expansion took place throughout Britain (see Source 3.14).

Because of the large sums of money involved, and the possible danger to life and limb, the Government felt forced to take some control. It passed a series of Acts to regulate the railways.

1840  Railway Regulating Act: Railways were put under the control of the Board of Trade, who appointed inspectors who had access to reports on traffic, charges and safety.

1844  Railway Act: This had three main parts:
a) Each company had to run 'Parliamentary Trains' daily over

## Source 3.14    The Railway network in Britain in 1845 and 1872.

1845

1872

## Source 3.15    Tay Bridge.

each line, stopping at each station, at a minimum speed of 12 mph.
b) The fare for 3rd class passengers was 1d (less than ½ new pence) per mile.
c) All carriages had to have doors, seats and windows.

1845  Gauge Act: All new railways had to be Standard Gauge (4ft 8½ins between the tracks).

1854  Railway & Canal Traffic Act: Railways were not to favour one customer with cheaper charges than another.

1873  Regulation of Railways Act: A commission was set up to decide on railway amalgamations and charges for cargoes.

This expansion required some major engineering works, such as the Tay Bridge, opened in 1878.

## Activities

1  Describe some of the difficulties which faced the early railway companies. **(KU)**

2  Which area(s) of Britain had fewest railways by 1872? **(KU)**

3  Study the list of Acts relating to railways, then copy and complete the table below, by putting a tick in each box that the Act tried to control. One example, the 1845 Gauge Act, is done for you. **(KU)**

|  | 1840 Act | 1844 Act | 1845 Act | 1854 Act | 1873 Act |
|---|---|---|---|---|---|
| Safety & Comfort |  |  |  |  |  |
| Traffic & Charges |  |  |  |  |  |
| Technical Problems |  |  | ✓ |  |  |

# The benefits of railways

The following sources give different views on railway travel between 1830 and 1844. In Source 3.16 Thomas Creevey describes travelling on the Liverpool and Manchester Railway in 1830.

## Source 3.16

*I had the satisfaction, for I can't call it pleasure, of taking a trip of five miles, at twenty miles an hour. It is really flying, and it is impossible to forget instant death coming to all if the least accident happens. It gave me a headache which has not yet left me.*

Seven years later, another passenger described the rail journey from Birmingham to Liverpool:

## Source 3.17

*At first I felt nervous and being run away with. But a sense of security soon came, and the speed was delightful. The view was a continually changing panorama. All other travelling is irksome and tedious by comparison.*

Some passengers did complain of the lack of comfort on the early third class trains. But Chambers' *Edinburgh Review* commented in 1844:

18

## Source 3.18

*The shabby rich, by using these trains, have only themselves to blame for being uncomfortable. We have been astounded to hear that men worth many thousands of pounds have used third class carriages on the Greenock Railway; some have even bought stools to sit on in these carriages.*

The 1844 Railway Act ensured that all carriages had to have seats, doors and windows; by the 1880s, the wealthy could hire private carriages, with a luggage compartment, private saloon, lavatory, pantry and a compartment for servants.

## Source 3.19

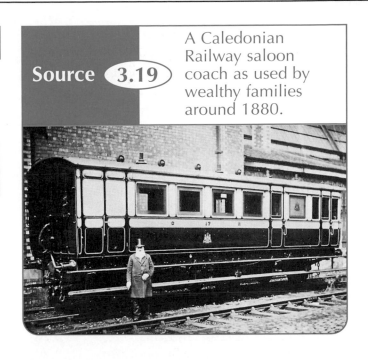

A Caledonian Railway saloon coach as used by wealthy families around 1880.

## Source 3.20 A locomotive built in 1865 for the North British Company.

Conditions for those who worked on the railways were often hard. Look at Source 3.20 to see how little protection drivers had. Also twelve hour days were common, as were accidents, and discipline was severe; any offence which affected a member of the public led to instant sacking. But jobs on the railways were eagerly sought. One reason was the low risk of unemployment, the other was the wage paid.

Railway wages in England were roughly double those in Scotland.

### Activities

1 Find out about rail travel.

   a) Which traveller did not enjoy rail travel, and why?

   b) Which one did? Again, give reasons for your choice. **(ENQ)**

2 What evidence is there that Chambers' 'Edinburgh Review' (Source 3.18) did not approve of rich people travelling third class? **(ENQ)**

3 Describe ways that passenger comfort improved by 1880. **(KU)**

| Source **3.21** | Average weekly wages paid in Scotland c.1843. | |  |
|---|---|---|---|

| Railways | | Others | |
|---|---|---|---|
| Drivers | £1.10 | Masons | £0.78 |
| Firemen | £0.65 | Wheelwrights | £0.70 |
| Guards | £0.95 | Weavers | £0.33 |
| Porters | £0.67 | Farm labourers | £0.45 |
| Gatekeepers | £0.70 | Casual labourers | £0.28 |

**Source 3.22** Transport in the 1830s, north and east of Glasgow.

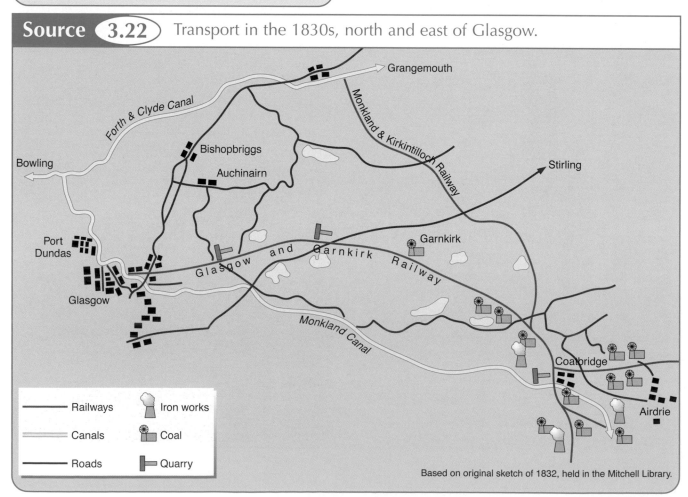

Based on original sketch of 1832, held in the Mitchell Library.

# The results of the railways

As early as 1832, industries soon grew up near the railways, as Source 3.22 above shows.

**Source 3.23** The great railway builder, Robert Stephenson, made this speech to the Institution of Civil Engineers in January 1856.

*The railways employ 90 400 officers and servants, while the engines consume annually two million tons of coal. In 1854, 111 million passengers were carried, each travelling an average of 12 miles.*

*The wear and tear is great. 20 000 tons of iron require to be replaced annually; 300 000 trees are annually felled to replace perished sleepers.*

*The postal facilities afforded by the railways are very great. Every Friday night, eight or ten vans are required to transport the weekly papers on the North Western Railway alone. Government papers would not be printed, for only the railways can transport them.*

He could also have mentioned the growth of holiday resorts, like Brighton or Ayr, or the growth of desirable suburbs near the main cities, from which the wealthy commuted. He could have mentioned the growth of railway towns, like Crewe or Kilmarnock, or the growth of exports of railway goods – by the end of the century, the Springburn district of Glasgow alone made one-quarter of the world's locomotives. Areas such as the Highlands were opened up to tourism.

When the Tay Bridge was opened, linking Newport with Dundee, William McGonagall wrote this poem in celebration.

**Source 3.24** 'The Newport Railway' by William McGonagall.

*Success to the Newport Railway,*
*Along the braes of the Silvery Tay,*
*And to Dundee straightway,*
*Across the Railway Bridge*
*o' the Silvery Tay,*
*Now the thrifty housewives of Newport*
*To Dundee will often resort,*
*Which will be to them profit and sport,*
*By bringing cheap tea, bread, and jam,*
*And also some of Lipton's ham,*
*Which will make their hearts feel light and gay,*
*And will cause them to bless the opening day*
*Of the Newport Railway.*

**Source 3.25** Lochawe Station and Hotel, 1880.

21

## Activities

**1** Does McGonagall's poem have any value as evidence about the effects of the railways? Explain your answer. **(ENQ)**

**Group Activity**
Get into groups of about four.
Read the section on the results of the railways again.
Then under each of the headings below, make lists of the effects that the coming of the railways had.
You are given an example under each heading to start you off.

◆ Jobs which were created on the railways e.g. **Signalmen**

◆ Industries which could sell their products to the railways e.g. **Clock-makers** (for time-keeping)

◆ Industries which could sell their products all over Britain e.g. **Slate quarries**

◆ Types of town which grew as a result of the railways e.g. **Dormitory towns** (for commuters)

◆ People/industries which suffered as more people went by rail e.g. **Private road companies** (turnpikes)

In the opinion of your group, was the growth of the railways important?
In making your decision, you should consider evidence such as

◆ who gained from railways

◆ who lost because of railways

◆ changes they made

◆ benefits to the whole country. **(KU)**

**Section A: 1830–80**

# Home and health

## Housing

A family's standard of living – how well off it is – is decided by the amount of money they have each week and how they spend it. In 1830 upper and middle class people lived in comfortable homes with many luxuries and servants to look after them.

### Life in the country

A room in a Victorian middle-class home.

People in the working class were not so lucky. They had to live near their work, often in a 'tied' house, that is, one owned by their employer. If they lost their jobs they were evicted from their homes.

In Scotland, unmarried male farm workers shared a room, often above the stable, while the women shared an attic or a room off the kitchen.

**Source 4.2** This piece is about a country cottage and was printed in the 'Morning Chronicle' in 1850.

*It is about 15 feet long, 10–12 feet wide . . . The walls are wet . . . there are 2 rooms . . . one below and the other above. In the fireplace is a small wood fire, over which hangs a pot . . . At one corner is a small rickety table. There are 3 old chairs and a stool or two. There is one room (for sleeping) and we counted nine in the family. The beds are large sacks filled with chaff . . . The clothes worn by the parents in the daytime make the main covering of the children by night.*

Married workers might have a good cottage like the one shown in Source 4.3.

**Source 4.3** The layout of a typical labourer's cottage from John Starforth 'The Architecture of the Farm', 1833.

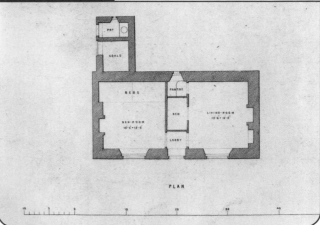

Some farm workers were given milk and oatmeal as part of their wages. They were also able to grow vegetables in their garden. However, for many, wages were low and they had trouble making ends meet. Source 4.4 is the weekly budget of a farm labourer in 1842.

**Source 4.4**

Weekly budget of Robert Crick, a farm labourer from Lavenham, Suffolk, c. 1842 published in the Reports on the Employment of Women and Children in Agriculture, Parliamentary Papers, 1843. (1s is 5 new pence and 1d is less than ½ new pence)

| Earnings | | |
|---|---|---|
| Robert Crick | (42 yrs) | 9s 0d |
| Wife | (40 " ) | 9d |
| Boy | (12 " ) | 2s 0d |
| " | (11 " ) | 1s 0d |
| " | ( 8 " ) | 1s 0d |
| Girl | ( 6 " ) | – |
| Boy | ( 4 " ) | – |
| | | 13s 9d |

| Expenditure | |
|---|---|
| Bread | 9s 0d |
| Potatoes | 1s 0d |
| Rent | 1s 2d |
| Tea | 2d |
| Sugar | 3½d |
| Soap | 3d |
| Blue | ½d |
| Thread etc. | 2d |
| Candles | 3d |
| Salt | ½d |
| Coal and wood | 9d |
| Butter | 4½d |
| Cheese | 3d |
| | 13s 9d |

## Life in the towns

Many ordinary townspeople lived in back to-back houses which often had only one room for the whole family to live in. This meant overcrowding was a problem. Look at source 4.5.

As much as three-quarters of a poor family's wage was spent on food. Their diet was dull and boring as shown by the account of Manchester cotton workers in 1833 in Source 4.6.

Sometimes bacon was added to potatoes and in really poor families children might have the bacon grease while father had the bacon. Many families could only afford to eat meat at Easter or Christmas and had to get the baker to cook it in his oven.

**Source 4.5** Urban overcrowding: a one-room family.

You can get an idea of what ordinary people might have eaten by looking at Source 4.6.

**Source 4.6**

**Mrs Gaskell**, 'The Manufacturing Population of England,' 1833.

*Their main food is potatoes and wheaten bread, washed down by tea or coffee. Meal (oatmeal) is eaten, either baked into cakes or boiled up with water, making a nourishing porridge which is easily digested and cooked. Animal food makes a very small part of their diet, and what they eat is often of poor quality. Fish is sometimes bought, usually herrings. Because these are salted they are difficult to digest. Eggs too make some part of their diet. The main food, however, is tea and bread.*

# Disease

The houses of ordinary working people were very poor in both country and town. Disease was more of a problem in towns for several reasons:

◆ overcrowding helped disease to spread;

◆ poor, or no, drains;

◆ up to 200 people might have to share one toilet, which was often just a hole in the ground.

As a result **epidemics** of diseases such as cholera caused many thousands of deaths. Look at the following table to see the kind of diseases which occurred frequently, especially in towns.

**Source 4.7**

| Disease | Causes | Symptoms | Results |
|---|---|---|---|
| cholera | tiny bacteria in water | cramps, diarrhoea, sickness, turn blue | coma and death in 50% of cases |
| typhoid | bad water and food | fever, diarrhoea, reddish rash | possible death |
| typhus | body lice, dirty houses, overcrowding | fever, headaches, rose-coloured rash | possible death |
| consumption/ tuberculosis | overcrowding, bad diet, poor ventilation | cough, spit blood, fever, waste away | death |

It was only when many thousands, poor and rich, died in epidemics that the Government started to take notice. In 1842 the Report on the Sanitary Conditions of the Labouring Population made certain recommendations. Some of these are given in Source 4.8.

**Source 4.8**

*The most important things needed are drains, removing rubbish from streets, purer water. There should be improved sewers and drains and a medical officer of health (doctor) should be put in charge of each district.*

In the Public Health Act 1848 towns were given powers to set up Boards of Health to see that all new houses had drains and lavatories and that houses were supplied with pure water. Although some towns did try to make improvements, a report from 1869 said that many towns were as bad as they had been in 1830.

## Activities

**1**  What two things help to give a family a good standard of living? **(KU)**

**2**  Imagine you are going to investigate people living in the nineteenth century. Think of **five** questions you can ask about their lives. One question is given to help you.

1.  Do you live in a town or in the country? **(ENQ)**

**3**  Compare homes in country and town by looking at Source 4.2 and Source 4.5 and filling out the chart below. Leave blanks if you do not have the information. **(ENQ)**

| Housing and health | | |
| --- | --- | --- |
| Aspect | Country | Town |
| No. People | 9 | 6 |
| No. Rooms | | |
| Repair | | |
| Lighting | | |
| Cooking | | |

**4**  Draw a circle and mark in it the part of their wages workers before 1850 spent on food, and what was left for everything else. **(KU)**

**5**  Look at Source 4.4 and 4.6. Describe what an average worker's family could have to eat. **(KU)**

**6**  Do you think this is a healthy diet? Explain your answer by thinking of the foods they do not eat. **(KU)**

**7**  Choose a house in **either** the country **or** the town.

a)  What diseases might the family in the house catch?

b)  Explain why.

c)  Why did families stay in such poor conditions in either town or country? **(KU)**

**8**  Study the table of killer diseases and the recommendations of the 1842 Report. (Source 4.8) Choose two recommendations and explain for **each**:

a)  What disease(s) it would fight.

b)  How it would help reduce the number of people killed. **(KU)**

**9**  Had any important reforms been introduced before 1850 to help improve living conditions in towns? **(KU)**

# Understanding disease

Doctors in the early nineteenth century did not know about germs and blamed epidemics, like the cholera epidemic of 1831–3 which killed 10 000 Scots, on 'miasmas' or 'effluvia', that is, smells floating around in the air. Although doctors didn't know the cause, their work showed them the sort of conditions where disease flourished, as Source 4.9, from the Report on the Sanitary Conditions of the Labouring Population 1842 shows.

Airdrie, a weaving town in the Lanarkshire coalfields, increased in population from 5000–14 000 between 1821 and 1846, with increasing problems of water supply. In 1846 towns in general had an average of seven grains of harmful substances per gallon of drinking water, but an analysis of water drunk in Airdrie in 1849 provided interesting reading, as shown in Source 4.9.

F/G LEVEL

CREDIT LEVEL

## Source 4.9

*Another problem in some parts of Edinburgh is the great size of the houses (some 10 storeys), with common stairs, sometimes as filthy as the streets onto which they open. The chance of cleanliness is lessened by the labour of carrying up water ... With Mr Chadwick, the police superintendent, and others, we visited a house at the back of the Canongate occupied by families of the labouring classes. A widow of respectable appearance, who answered some of our questions, occupied a room above a pigsty. ... On the occasion of the dungheap being removed from the pigsty, two children who lived with her, a daughter and a niece, were made ill by the effluvia from below, and both died within a few days.*

## Source 4.10

| Source of water | Total amount in grains of harmful insoluble matter in 1 gallon | Substances found in water |
|---|---|---|
| Town well Motherwell's | 56 | iron |
| well | 46 | |
| County jail | 84 | |
| National bank | 134 | natural waste, iron |
| Clarkston pit | 46 | iron |
| Clarkston spring | 8 | natural waste, iron |
| Rawyards pit | 38 | iron |
| Rawyards spring | 22 | iron |

Large cities like London had enormous problems with polluted water supplies, as Source 4.10 shows.

## Source 4.11

This is a cartoon from the magazine 'Punch' in the 1850s which draws attention to pollution in the River Thames.

A DROP OF LONDON WATER.

# Improvements in health and housing

A report published in 1869 revealed that many towns were as unhealthy as they had been in the 1830s. As a result Public Health Acts in 1872 and 1875 tried to set minimum standards for health and sanitation throughout Britain. These included the following:

◆ Local councils had to lay sewers, drains and pavements, provide street cleansing and provide towns with street lighting and fire services.

◆ Medical Officers of Health were appointed to deal with infections and take measures to cope with disease and stop it spreading.

27

◆ Sanitary inspectors not only made sure that streets and buildings were kept clean – they could also seize contaminated food and destroy it.

◆ Councils could provide water and lavatories where necessary and they could build baths and wash-houses to help people keep clean.

These improvements were more difficult to carry out in the older parts of towns, so the Artisans' Dwelling Act of 1875, which allowed councils to take over and demolish slum areas, was very important. It gave councils powers they could use when they found money for improvements.

## Activities

1 Look at Sources 4.1 to 4.5. Was life in towns better for people than life in the countryside in the middle of the nineteenth century? Give reasons to support you opinion. **(KU)**

2 What were the main causes of disease in the middle of the nineteenth century? **(KU)**

3 Explain why Source 4.9 is valuable as evidence about ill-health in cities like Edinburgh in the middle of the nineteenth century. **(ENQ)**

4 Study Source 4.10.

   a) Do you think it was healthy to drink water in places like Airdrie. Give reasons for your answer. **(KU)**

   b) Why do you think it was so bad? **(KU)**

5 Cartoons often exaggerate because they are trying to win people over to their viewpoint. How can you tell Source 4.11 is exaggerating? **(ENQ)**

6 What does the author of Source 4.11 think about London's water supply in the 1850s? **(ENQ)**

7 How important were the laws on public health passed in the 1870s? **(KU)**

8 Use materials from your class and school library to find out about one of the cholera epidemics in Scotland between 1831 and 1854. Write a short paragraph explaining how local authorities dealt with it. **(INV)**

# 5 Privilege, power and the people

## Towards democracy

### What is democracy?

Democracy has been called 'government of the people, by the people, for the people'. It is a system of government where people of a country freely elect representatives to make laws to benefit everybody. Britain in the nineteenth century was not a democracy, despite the 1832 reform of parliament.

### The Government of Britain in the mid-nineteenth century

In 1850 Britain was ruled by the Monarch, Queen Victoria, and Parliament, which was made up of the House of Commons and the House of Lords. All the members of the House of Lords came from the aristocracy and were not elected by ordinary people. The House of Commons was made up of men who were elected, but only by a small number of people – all men! Parliament passed Bills which were then agreed by the monarch and became Acts of Parliament and the laws of the country.

All the members of both the House of Commons and House of Lords were men and were also landowners or rich businessmen who passed laws mainly to suit themselves. The people who elected them – the voters – were also all men and were either landowners, tenant farmers, professional men, like doctors or lawyers, or businessmen. At elections, voters had to say in public which candidate they were voting for.

At elections people voted in public for the candidates so it was possible to bribe or force voters to choose particular candidates. Many people objected to this system which was called 'open voting'. For example a tenant farmer could lose his farm if he did not vote for the candidate his landlord wanted. In other cases voters were given beer or spirits to win over their vote or to make them too drunk to use it! Look at Source 5.2 to see what open voting was like.

Many of those who did not have the vote – such as businessmen and working class people in towns and the countryside – did not like the way the country was run and how members of Parliament were elected. From 1851 trade unions of skilled workers tried to show politicians that they deserved the right to vote, partly because they were becoming better and better educated. They convinced some members of Parliament and on the 12th April 1866 W. E. Gladstone, who was the leader of the Liberal Party, made the following speech.

### Source 5.1

*Since 1832 education has been brought to the mass of the people. Newspapers are circulated by the million. The self-improving powers of the working community [are shown by] the Working Men's Free Libraries and Institutes . . . There are now 650 000 depositors in the Post Office Savings Banks . . . What is the meaning of all this? Parliament has been striving to make the working classes fitter and fitter for the franchise . . .*

**Source** 5.2   Open voting at the Hustings: the method of voting before 1872.

In the 1860s the Liberal Party was in power. It gained most of its support from merchants and industrialists and thought that landowners had too much power. The Liberal leader, Lord John Russell, introduced a bill in parliament to give more MPs to towns and cities. Some of his own Party disagreed with him and he resigned.

There were huge meetings in London and other cities demanding reform so when the Conservatives took over they passed The 1867 Parliamentary Reform Act.

## Reform of Parliament 1867 to 1918

In 1867 a Parliamentary Reform Act was passed by which the right to vote was given to all male householders in the boroughs and to lodgers paying £10 a year rent. In the counties, £12 leaseholders (those renting land) had the vote.

The Act also took account of the migration of the population by taking 45 seats from boroughs of less than 10 000 people and redistributing them, giving 25 seats to the counties and the rest to large towns.

This act meant that the number of voters almost doubled to just under 2 million, all men, with most of the new voters being skilled workers in the towns. In elections, politicians had to hold big meetings to try to win over voters. Landowners, however, still had too much power in the counties.

In 1872 the secret ballot was introduced to the delight of people such as the anonymous writer of this letter to the editor of *Reynoldson's Newspaper*.

## Source 5.3

*Sir,*
*With the ballot, farmers will be better able to return a different set of men to the House of Commons. Hitherto, farmers have been compelled to vote for a candidate of the landlords. Hence it is that county members of parliament are generally landowners, and their kinsfolk and . . . supporters. The landowners stink and swarm in Parliament and are a nuisance to be got rid of. We shall not have honest laws until many landowners are replaced by working men.*
*A Warwickshire Labourer*

This was the new way of voting.

## Source 5.4

Voting by ballot, after 1872.

It was 1884 before another Reform Act extended male household suffrage to the counties, raising the number of voters from 2 to 5 million.

However, Britain was still not a full democracy because women, male domestic servants and others still did not have the vote.

Since MPs did not receive wages, only rich men could enter parliament. The House of Lords, which was not elected, could stop the elected House of Commons from passing new laws.

Many working class people wanted votes for all adult men. Now that most children went to school, working class people could read newspapers and many were unhappy they did not have the same rights as the rich. Workers used trade unions to fight for better wages and working conditions, but they found they needed new laws passed. When the Liberals and Conservatives did not help enough, the Labour Representation Committee was set up in 1900 to help get working men elected to parliament. In 1906 their 23 MPs decided to call themselves the Labour Party.

They had little chance of making up a government until the vote was given to all adult men. This did not happen until the end of the First World War, 1918.

## Activities

1 Who had the right to vote in 1850? **(KU)**

2 Explain

   a) why changes were made to voting rights in 1867.

   b) the actual changes to voting made in 1867. **(KU)**

3 What further changes were made to voting in 1884? **(KU)**

4 Discuss the attitude of the writer of Source 5.3 to reform of Parliament. **(ENQ)**

5 Explain the importance of the 1872 Ballot Act. **(KU)**

6 How democratic was Britain by 1884? **(KU)**

GENERAL/CREDIT LEVEL

# 6 Enquiry Skills: Investigating

At Foundation level you will be expected to be able to use enquiry skills to work with historical evidence. You should be able to do three things with sources you are given on a topic:

◆ support an opinion on one of the sources presented to you;

◆ write down relevant evidence on the topic from the sources;

◆ write down what you think you have found out about the topic you are investigating.

Here is an example of an investigation.

The topic under investigation is:

---

## Working conditions in coal mines in the 1840s

*Study the information in the sources, then answer the questions which follow.*

**Source A** is from a speech given to parliament by Lord Londonderry, the owner of a large coal mine, in June 1842.

### Source A

*The trappers' job is neither cheerless nor dull. Nor is the trapper without light. The trapper is generally cheerful and contented and to be found, like other children of his age, busy with some childish amusement – like cutting sticks, drawing figures with chalk on the door or modelling figures in clay.*

**1** Give two reasons why **Source A** is useful evidence for investigating working conditions in mines in the 1840s.

Reason 1 _____

Reason 2 _____

*2 marks*

**Source B** is from a report on the Collieries and Iron-works in the East of

Scotland published by the Children's Employment Commission in 1842. This particular evidence comes from John Savile aged 6.

### Source B

*I stand and open and shut the door; I'm generally in the dark, and I sit down against the door; I stay twelve hours in the pit; I never see daylight, except on Sunday; I fell asleep one day and a cart ran over my leg and made it hurt.*

**2** Look at Sources A and B.

What does Source A tell us about working conditions in mines?

What does Source B tell us about conditions in some other mines?

*4 marks*

**3** Write your findings on whether working conditions in mines were bad in the 1840s.

*2 marks*

Here are some guidelines to help you answer the questions.

1   To answer the first question you need to think about such things as:

*What type of evidence is Source A? Because it comes from the same time as the mine it describes it is called* **primary evidence** *and you should say this.*

*It comes from a person who might be biased because he is a mine owner and might think improvements would cut down his profits or make it more difficult to work his coal mine.*

*It gives several pieces of relevant information about work in mines – but all are about good features of mines.*

In your answer you should mention any **two** of the above pieces of evidence.

2   The second question has **4** marks, so you will need to find four pieces of relevant evidence. **Make sure you use both sources by selecting at least one piece of evidence from each** – even if you think there are four pieces in just one source.

**Source A** tells you that in this mine:

◆   *trappers were not without light;*

◆   *children were cheerful and contented;*

◆   *children played with chalk or clay.*

You should write down **two** of the above pieces of evidence.

**Source B** tells you that in another mine:

◆   *children were in the dark;*

◆   *children worked 12 hours and did not see daylight during the week;*

◆   *a child was hurt when a cart ran over his leg.*

Again, write down **two** pieces of evidence from the source.

3   In your answer to item 3 do not just write 'I think working conditions were bad.' If you do you may get no marks.

Instead you might write **EITHER**:

I think working conditions were bad in some mines because a little boy had to stand in the dark for a long time, opening and shutting a door and never seeing daylight and sometimes accidents happened. But the other source says the trappers had lights and were happy, so maybe things were not bad in all mines.

**OR**

I think working conditions were bad in mines because of what the little boy says in Source B about being in the dark and being hurt and because I do not believe what the mine owner says in Source A as he might not tell the truth.

**Remember!! You can also use other evidence you know about from your teacher or sources you have seen elsewhere to support what you think.**

# 7 Changing Britain

## Society Around 1900

British society before the First World War was split into classes as it had been all through the nineteenth century. Which class you belonged to depended on:

- who your parents were;
- how rich they were;
- what job they did.

The next source gives you some information about the different classes in Britain at this time.

### Source 7.1

| Class | % Population | Jobs | Yearly Income |
|---|---|---|---|
| UPPER | 0.5 | landowners | £2000 + |
| MIDDLE Upper | 2.5 | bankers, industrialists, judges, doctors | £1000–2000 |
| Lower | 17.0 | shopkeepers, clerks, teachers | £150–500 |
| WORKING Skilled | 80.0 | engineers, joiners, foremen | £100–150 |
| Unskilled | | labourers | £35–55 |

By 1900 almost three out of four of the people in Britain lived in the towns and cities. The better off classes lived in comfort as can be seen from the picture of a room from 1895, shown in Source 7.2 on the next page.

Improvements for the working class came very slowly. Compulsory education, trade unions and the First World War led to votes for all and forced political parties to support more social reform, as the working class now made up the biggest number of voters.

## Population movement and emigration

By the 1870s, competition from abroad was making sheep farming less profitable in Britain. Some Highland landlords turned their lands into sporting estates, so the rich could come and shoot grouse or deer. This meant even less work for Highlanders on these estates. By the 1880s many crofters were unwilling to let landlords evict them and police and troops were brought from the south of Scotland to keep law and order. The Government heard evidence about problems in the Highlands from people like John MacPherson of Skye, part of whose evidence to the Napier Commission is given in Source 7.3 on page 35.

**Source 7.2**  The better-off classes lived in comfort: a drawing room as it would have appeared in 1895.

**Source 7.3** John MacPherson in the Napier Commission Report.

*With more families sharing the hill, pasture grazing is scarce and people suffer badly. Instead of the milk now they only have treacle and tea to wash down the food. Our staple food is meal, potatoes, fish when it is got . . . I don't think we have more than five or six (hens). If we had more we would have to buy feeding for them.*

*Our houses in rainy weather are most deplorable. Above our beds comes pattering down the rain . . . Of the 20 houses there are only two in which the cattle are not under the same roof as the family.*

In 1886 the Government passed the Crofters' Holding Act which gave the crofters the 'three Fs'. These were fair rent, decided by a land court called the Crofters' Commission; fixed tenure, which meant that they could not be evicted as long as they paid their rent; freedom of a son to inherit his father's land.

These changes did not protect those without land and the population of the crofting areas dropped from 180 000 in 1881 to 120 000 in 1931. Some went south to the towns but many others went abroad to Canada, Australia, New Zealand or South Africa, and around 50 per cent of Scots emigrants went to the USA.

FOUNDATION/GENERAL LEVEL

Between 1904 and 1913 some 600 000 people, around 13 per cent of the total Scottish population, sailed overseas.

From the 1870s there was also migration from Scottish mining areas to England and Wales, though this slowed after 1900. Emigration dropped during the First World War but rose again in the difficult years of the 1920s. The world trade depression from 1930 meant there was little opportunity for Scots going to other countries.

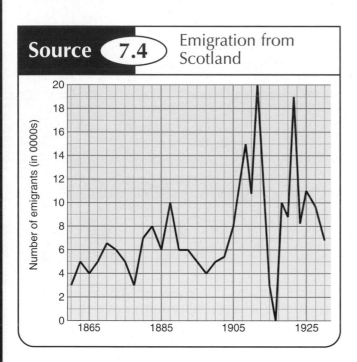

**Source 7.4** Emigration from Scotland

Number of emigrants (in 0000s)

## Immigration

Between 1880 and the early 1900s, some 25 000 people came from Italy, Russia and Baltic states like Lithuania to settle in Scotland. Some Italians left poverty and unemployment to find better lives for themselves. The Lithuanians left higher taxes and poverty to come to the coal mines of Lanarkshire, hoping to use it as a first step on the way to America. Others left Russia because the government of their homeland used secret police to spy on workers so they could imprison anyone

who wished to fight for trade unions or democracy. Some were Jewish and left eastern Europe after they were persecuted because of their religion.

### Activities

1 Study Source 7.1.
Draw a circle with a radius of 5 cm. Colour it in showing the percentage of people in the three main classes. **(KU)**

2 What changes forced governments to pay more attention to the conditions of the working class? **(KU)**

3 Why did many people leave the Highlands after 1880? **(KU)**

4 Was emigration or immigration more important in changing the population of Scotland between 1880–1939? Explain your answer. **(KU)**

## The economy

At the end of the nineteenth century, Britain ruled an empire covering almost one-quarter of the world. From the 1850s onwards her industry and trade were so strong she regarded herself as 'the workshop of the world'. She was able to sell her goods more cheaply than other countries and this meant cheaper goods at home, high profits for businessmen and an improvement in wages for the workers.

People in Britain thought this would continue and few noticed any worrying signs. Britain's main industries were:

◆ coal

◆ textiles (cotton and wool)

◆ iron and steel

◆ heavy engineering.

By the end of the century, the USA was the

world's leading producer of coal. By 1908, Germany was producing twice as much steel as Britain.

Britain fell further behind her competitors because of the First World War, which cost so much to fight and lost many customers for British goods. British industries were slow to invest money in things like oil and electricity and this made it more difficult to compete with other countries.

# Urbanisation

Despite emigration, the population of Britain was growing by about 1 per cent per year and by 1900, large towns were expanding so quickly they were swallowing up villages near them.

**Source 7.5**

The historian T. C. Smout offers some explanation for this continuing trend in the twentieth century in 'A Century of the Scottish People, 1850–1950'.

*As the century passed, the culture of the cities came to dominate the culture of the countryside, through the popular press and radio, and rural ways seemed narrow and dull to the young. Farm work appeared as a rough, dirty, badly paid job with long hours and few holidays.*

Census figures show us that between 1871 and 1900 the number of British towns of over 100 000 rose from 14 to 33.

**Source 7.6** Census data

| | 1801 | 1851 | 1901 |
|---|---|---|---|
| London | 957 000 | 2 362 000 | 4 536 000 |
| Birmingham | 71 000 | 233 000 | 523 000 |
| Manchester | 70 000 | 303 000 | 645 000 |
| Liverpool | 82 000 | 376 000 | 704 000 |
| Sheffield | 46 000 | 135 000 | 407 000 |
| Glasgow | 77 000 | 329 000 | 776 000 |
| Cardiff | – | 18 000 | 164 000 |

## Change and the Working Class

Poverty was still common among the working class but education, which had been made compulsory in 1870 in England and 1872 in Scotland, was slowly bringing changes. Working class newspapers like the *Daily Mail* (1896) and the *News of the World* had a circulation of over a million and gave short articles on crime, sport and other news. Although they simplified issues, they were capable of influencing public opinion and the politicians. The Liberal Government of 1906–14 found themselves passing reforms to stop working class voters changing over to the new Labour Party.

Trade Union membership, which had been 4 million in 1914, rose to 8.3 million by 1920. Despite the failure of the General Strike in 1926, the partnership of Trade Unions and Labour Party helped bring about social reform. The trade depression of the 1930s, with 22 per cent unemployment in 1932, slowed down improvements in the standard of living but there was no doubt parliament now had to be responsible to the whole nation, not just a privileged minority.

## Activities

1 In what ways was Britain a strong, influential country in the second half of the nineteenth century? **(KU)**

2 Why had her position changed by the end of the 1930s? **(KU)**

3 What important change took place in the distribution of population in Britain by the end of the nineteenth century? **(KU)**

4 Describe some of the important changes for working class people between 1880 and 1932. For this answer you should write a short essay of several paragraphs **(KU)**

Section B: 1880–1940

CREDIT LEVEL

# 8 Changes on the land

Between 1870 and 1914 the number of people employed in agriculture fell by 25 per cent, while the population rose by 40 per cent. Wheat prices fell from 55s (£2.75) per quarter in 1870 to 33s (£1.65) in 1914, and only 7s (35p) in 1939. The area growing wheat fell from 3.6m acres in 1872 to 1.7m acres in 1914, and stayed at that level in 1939, despite the wartime rise to 2.6m acres.

The Government set up two Royal Commissions to examine the problem, in 1879 and 1893. Their findings were:

◆ Foreign competition: transport developments, especially steamships and railways, meant that cheap food, mainly wheat and refrigerated meat, flooded into Britain.

◆ New foods: traditional foods like butter were facing competition from substitutes like margarine.

◆ Bad weather: six wet summers, between 1873 and 1879, reduced crops when farmers needed them most. In 1879 alone, sheep rot, brought on by the wet weather, caused the death of 3 million sheep.

There was little the Government could do, because it did not want to abandon the policy of Free Trade. (This allowed foreign goods into the country free of taxes; other countries did the same for British manufactured goods.) Also, the bulk of the population was benefitting from cheaper food prices – a 4lb loaf cost 7d in 1880, 6d in 1890 and only 5½d in 1900 (1d is less than ½ new pence). Falling food prices meant that people could afford to eat better – meat, milk, butter and vegetable consumption all rose steadily.

**Source 8.1** Lord Ernle gave his view of the problems facing farmers in 'English Farming, Past and Present,' 1927.

*Parliament did not give any help or protection to agriculture. The policy of Free Trade was too important, as it brought cheap food to the working class; there were no tariffs brought in to protect agriculture. Thrown on their own resources, agriculturalists fought the unequal contest with courage, but with weakening resources. Land got into poorer condition; fewer workers were employed.*

Many years later the historian G. M. Trevelyan gave more information about the problems British farmers faced in the late nineteenth century, particularly from overseas competition.

**Source 8.2** — Trevelyan's 'English Social History', 1944.

*From 1875 catastrophe set in. A series of bad harvests made the situation worse, but the cause was the development of the American prairies as farm lands. New agricultural machinery let farmers cultivate the unlimited lands of the American Mid-West; railroads carried the produce to ports; steamers carried it to Britain. Mass-production of crops by a simpler and cheaper process undercut the elaborate and expensive methods of farming built up on well-managed estates over the past two hundred years.*

*Landlords and farmers complained in vain. The belief in Free Trade, the dominance of the towns over the country, memories of the 'hungry forties' when the Corn Laws made bread too dear for the poor – all these prevented any effort to save farming.*

Farmers who changed to products such as fruit and vegetables prospered. The area growing fruit doubled between 1873 and 1907. Grassland for animals and poultry increased by 6 million acres in the same period, while acres under wheat and barley only fell by 2 million. The numbers of livestock rose.

**Source 8.3** — Figures from P. Matthias, 'The First Industrial Nation.'

| Year | Cattle | Sheep | Pigs | Horses |
|------|--------|-------|------|--------|
| 1872 | 5.6m | 27.9m | 2.7m | 1.2m |
| 1913 | 6.9m | 23.9m | 2.2m | 1.3m |
| 1939 | 8.1m | 25.9m | 3.7m | 0.9m |

## Activities

1 How important were changes in technology as the reason for the decline in British agriculture after the 1870s? Justify your answer. **(KU)**

2 Was all agriculture in trouble after 1880? Again, explain your answer. **(KU)**

3 How far does Ernle's attitude towards these changes agree with Trevelyan's **(KU)**?

# Farming and the first world war

When war broke out in 1914, the importance of agriculture was soon realised. In that year, Britain produced only one-fifth of the wheat needed. If supplies of food from overseas were cut off, Britain would soon starve.

The Government immediately took steps to grow more food. Areas that had been grassland were ploughed up. Allotments were started so that people could grow some food themselves; city parks and even golf courses were turned into vegetable patches.

The biggest problem was getting people to work on the land. Many men had joined the armed forces. Posters like this one appeared in 1915 and after.

**Source 8.4** Poster encouraging women to join the Land Army.

As a result, many women started working on the land, ploughing, sowing, hoeing, harvesting and driving tractors. Without women like these, Britain would have starved.

**Source 8.5** Land Army women working in an Essex cornfield.

The Government also controlled wages and prices. Food production soon increased. Wheat and potato output rose by 60 per cent. The people of Britain ate better than those of Germany, where they suffered severe food shortages.

When the war ended, agriculture was less important. Government controls ended. Both prices and wages fell sharply. People left the land in growing numbers, looking for a better life in the cities, or abroad.

## Changes on the land

After the war, agriculture's decline continued. In Scotland between 1921 and 1938 farm output fell from £48m to £40m; the number of farm workers fell from 126 900 to 105 300. A new reason for this decline was a change in government policy. Subsidies paid for sugar beet (after 1925) and wheat (after 1932) benefitted the South and East of England; only 6 per cent of the subsidies went to Scotland. Many Scottish farmers decided to try their luck in the south.

Those who stayed made the best of it. Some tried to introduce new machinery, like that in Source 8.7.

**Source 8.6** Is a comment from Ronald Blythe, a Scottish farmer from Akenfield.

*News about East Anglia got about fast. A better climate, easier working soil, with no damn great lumps of granite pushing out of it.*

CREDIT LEVEL

**Source** 8.7 A tractor pulling a reaper-binder in 1936.

The Government did take some action to help the dwindling number of farm labourers. In 1924 it set up a board to recommend minimum wage levels for farm labourers. This recognised their poor bargaining position; even so, they remained among the poorest paid in Britain.

## Activities

1   What was done to increase Britain's food output in wartime? **(KU)**

2   Why was the work of the Women's Land Army important? **(KU)**

3   What effects did the end of the war have on farming? **(KU)**

4   Why did some Scottish farmers move south in the 1930s? **(KU)**

# 9 Industry

For Scotland's industries, this was a period of two very different stories. Up until 1914, Scotland was the home of prosperous heavy industries; after the First World War, these industries were in difficulties.

## Coal

In the years between 1880 and 1914, coal mining became Britain's biggest industry. It employed over one million men and exported a record amount of coal to other countries. Cardiff overtook Newcastle to become the world's biggest exporter of coal.

| Source 9.1 | | Coal production | |
| --- | --- | --- | --- |
| | Total Output (million tons) | Exports (m. tons) | Employment (thousands) |
| 1880 | 156 | 20 | 504 |
| 1910 | 270 | 65 | 1094 |
| 1930 | 220 | 43 | 780 |

Working conditions remained dangerous. In the years 1922 to 1924, no less than 597 198 miners were injured. The figures do not include those off work for less than seven days! Boys as young as 14 were legally allowed to work underground in this most dangerous industry, as the photograph in Source 9.2 shows.

**Source 9.2** A young boy working in the mines.

There were no facilities at the pit head. Miners had to bathe and dry their clothes once they walked home; this was sometimes three miles away.

**Source 9.3** A miner bathing.

**Source 9.4**   Clothes drying at the fireside.

After the end of the First World War, many miners faced hard times. British coal was more expensive than coal from other countries. Mine owners saw only one way to make British coal cheaper, and that was to cut wages and make miners work longer hours. After many arguments, the miners' union called a strike in 1926. They got great support from other unions who called a General Strike of all workers for nine

days. Britain came to a halt. After the other workers were called back to work by their own unions, the miners remained on strike until they were starved back to work after six months. They had to accept longer hours and less pay.

Things got even worse after 1929. A slump in world trade, known as the Depression, meant that other industries could not sell their goods, so they stopped buying coal. For the next 10 years many miners were out of work.

## Activities

1   What shows that coal mining was an important industry between 1880 and 1930? **(KU)**

2   What evidence is there that working in the mines was

   a)   unpleasant

   b)   dangerous? **(KU)**

3   Do the figures in Source 9.1 show that coal mining was in trouble after the First World War (1914–18)? Give two pieces of evidence to support your answer. **(KU)**

4   Why is Source 9.2 valuable evidence of working conditions in mines between 1880 and 1939? Give at least two reasons for your answer. **(ENQ)**

# New technology and foreign competition

The figures in Source 9.1 show that mining expanded to a peak in the years immediately before the First World War, and declined after that. The reasons for the expansion were the continued growth of the industries which were coal's best customers, like cotton and the railways,

and the arrival of new industries like chemicals and steamships. Also, as Britain owned 80 per cent of the world's merchant ships, it was easier to export coal from Britain. In addition, coal from South Wales was the best in the world for warships, as it burned with very little smoke, and foreign navies bought it.

The huge increase in output was not achieved by improvements in technology.

More mechanical cutting equipment was used, but most British coal seams were less than 1 metre thick, too shallow to make them worthwhile. Most of the increase came about by expanding the workforce – employing more miners.

Given the importance of coal, it was in this period that miners were most successful in improving their wages and hours of work – often after bitter strikes.

## Coal mining after the First World War

It was the First World War that changed mining. There was a desperate need for more coal to power the munitions and other industries. Coal was dug from the best remaining seams, without any thought of conserving reserves for the future; maintenance of equipment was neglected. The industry was in poor shape to meet the competition from countries like Germany and Poland which were desperately exporting coal to earn the money they needed. The war had also hastened other developments. The expansion of cars and lorries hit the railways, one of coal's best customers. The growth of the electricity industry was another threat. Miners returning from the war had hoped for a better life, but were faced with demands from the coal owners for wage cuts and longer hours as the only way to make British coal sell. Attempts by the owners to force these changes on the miners led to a bitter six-month strike in 1926, which the miners lost.

Any benefit the owners got from cutting wages and lengthening shifts disappeared when the Great Depression started in 1929. The worst hit industries were mainly coal's best customers – the railways, cotton, iron and steel, and shipbuilding. Things only got better after about 1937, when the government decided to rearm to face Hitler, and demand for ships, iron and steel benefited coal.

More evidence about problems facing coal mining after the First World War is given in Source 9.5 by the historian M. W. Flynn.

**Source 9.5** An Economic and Social History of Britain since 1700.

*Labour in the mines remained cheap; there was little incentive for mine owners to equip mines with mechanical cutters.*

*Electricity began to compete effectively with coal in both the home and factory.*

*Governments of foreign coal-producing countries began subsidising their exports; Britain lost markets such as Scandinavia.*

*Mine owners tried to cut wages in order to cut costs; this caused a series of disputes, the most serious being in 1926, when the miners were on strike for six months.*

Another view was given by a Conservative MP:

**Source 9.6** Sir Leo Money MP, 1918.

*The inefficiency of British industries is by no means only due to the workers who have tried to limit output, but also to the manufacturers and to the Government. British employers have been too conservative. They have ignored new techniques and inventions, they have relied for success on cheap labour rather than on the greatest efficiency in organisation.*

CREDIT LEVEL

F/G LEVEL

## Activities
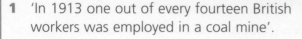

1   'In 1913 one out of every fourteen British workers was employed in a coal mine'.

**Either**

a)  Explain the success of coal mining in Britain before the First World War

**or**

b)  Explain the decline of the coal industry after the First World War.
    (In each case you should write a short essay of several paragraphs.) **(KU)**

# Shipbuilding

Shipbuilding was an industry that grew quickly between 1880 and 1939. This was mainly because of the huge growth of Britain's trade with overseas countries.

**Source** **9.7**  This photograph shows Alexander Hall's shipyard in Aberdeen in 1880.

There were several changes in the way ships were built. Around 1880, wooden ships were becoming rare; newer ships were built of iron, and later, steel. Steamships were replacing sailing ships, because they did not depend on a good wind. Lastly, ships were becoming larger, so they could sail further, and carry more.

Working in shipyards was dangerous and hard.

**Source** **9.8**  This extract comes from 'The Govan Press', 24 August 1900.

*Shortly before 10 o'clock on Friday morning, John Connolly, a ship-plater, lost his life at Fairfield Shipbuilding Yard. While climbing a ladder into the boilerhold he overbalanced and fell 32 feet. Two other accidents also occurred in the Fairfield Yards. Charles Scott, 17, a template boy, fell from the top of a ladder – 30 feet – and suffered serious injuries to his neck and back; and John Miller, a plater, lost two of the fingers of his left hand by a steel plate falling on them.*

A major complaint of the men was the lack of job security they had. They could be laid off at only two hours' notice. They tried to improve their position by jealously guarding their own craft; for example, joiners worked on wood less than 4cm thick, but carpenters did the work if it was over that thickness. These rules agreed between crafts were called demarcation. Management often called them 'restrictive practices'.

## Source 9.9 — Shipyards on the Clyde.

### Activities

1 In what three ways did the building of ships change between 1880–1939? **(KU)**

2 What differences are there between the shipyards shown in Sources 9.7 and 9.9? **(KU)**

3 Why is Source 9.8 good evidence about dangers in shipyards? **(ENQ)**

# Good times, bad times for shipbuilding

Scotland benefited more than most areas from the growth of shipbuilding. It had cheap steel, skilled workers and deep sheltered rivers for launching. This was one reason why Yarrows moved from London to the Clyde in 1906. Many Scottish firms gained from the big expansion of the Royal Navy between 1906 and 1914. By this time, one-fifth of the world's ships were built in Scotland.

The Clyde in particular was lined with shipyards from Glasgow to Dumbarton, and with more at Greenock and Port Glasgow.

When the First World War ended in 1918, the good times continued. Shipowners in this country rushed to replace ships that had been sunk in the war. But by 1921, the stream of orders dried up. The 1920s were hard. Many shipyard workers were laid off.

In 1929 came worse news. After the **Wall Street Crash** in America came a Great Depression in world trade. No-one needed new ships. Shipyards closed all over the country. Probably the worst-hit town was Jarrow, near Newcastle; it depended on Palmer's Shipyard, the town's only industry. The yard got no orders at all in 1932. To help the industry out of its difficulties, a group of yard owners formed a company called the National Shipbuilding Security Ltd. It bought up yards in order to share out the few orders going. In 1934 it bought Palmer's and closed it down.

CREDIT LEVEL

## Source 9.10

A Special Correspondent of **The Times** newspaper reported the closure of Palmer's shipyard on the 21 March 1934 as follows.

*One feels, sometimes strongly and angrily, that London still has no idea of the troubles that face the industrial north. In London and the South, for every 84 men working, there are 14 out of work. In Jarrow, a formerly prosperous town of 32000 inhabitants, for every 25 working, there are 75 out.*

Scotland suffered almost as badly. Groups of unemployed men hung about street corners, as shown in Source 9.11.

## Source 9.11

In 1939 the Scottish Economic Committee summed up the situation.

## Source 9.12

*Shipbuilding occupies a key position, both in itself, and through the dependence on it of the steel industry and others down to the furniture needed for passenger vessels. Any contraction in world trade has a depressing effect not only on shipbuilding, but on a whole group of industries. A further difficulty is subsidised competition from foreign shipbuilding industries. Rising costs, partly due to rearmament, threaten to end any orders for merchant shipping.*

Government help ensured that the 'Queen Mary' was completed by John Brown's of Clydebank.

### Activities

1   Show evidence that shipbuilding was an important industry in the period 1880–1939? **(KU)**

2   Was the Special Correspondent of 'The Times' sympathetic to the problems of areas which depended on shipbuilding? Explain your answer. **(ENQ)**

# Women and work

At the beginning of the twentieth century, the most common job for women was as a domestic servant. Writing about Women's Rights in 1971 one author describes their working conditions around 1900.

| Source 9.13 | An extract from 'Women's Rights,' 1971. |
|---|---|

*There were no labour-saving devices, and they usually worked a grinding day of about fourteen hours. Many were housed in cold cramped attics, fed on left-overs, and allowed only half a day free a fortnight.*

Even worse off were those who worked as seamstresses, making up clothes. They were paid 1p an hour and had to pay for their own needles, thread and candles! Many people at the time called this a 'sweated trade'; to earn enough to live, they had to work 16 hours a day, every day.

Women also worked in heavier jobs, such as brick-making and chain-making.

| Source 9.14 | These women were employed in heavy industry. |
|---|---|

Perhaps worst off of all were the girls who made matches. Their working conditions are described in the next source.

| Source 9.15 | John Simkin described the conditions Annie Besant found at Bryant & May's factory in London in 'Trade Unions 1800–1918'. |
|---|---|

*Wages were as low as 20p per week. However they did not always receive their full wage because of a system of fines, ranging from 2p to 5p. Offences included dropping matches and answering back. Besant also discovered that the health of the women had been severely affected by the phosphorus that they used to make the matches.*

Even doing the same jobs as men, the half million women working in Britain's industries earned less than half the pay of men. It was only at the beginning of the twentieth century that women were allowed into professions such as medicine and teaching. But even then women teachers who married had to give up their jobs.

## Activities

1  In what four ways was life as a domestic servant hard? **(KU)**

2  What complaints did women match workers at Bryant & May have about

   a) their wages

   b) factory discipline

   c) dangers to health? **(KU)**

3  Many women at this time claimed they were treated unfairly at work. Find as much evidence as you can to support this view. **(KU)**

49

# The changing position of women

By 1939 the position of women had improved overall. There were several reasons for this:

1  The growth of education; the Acts of 1902 and 1918 extended opportunities for education. They also created a need for more teachers. In Scotland in 1914, 65 per cent of teachers were women – but male teachers were paid almost twice as much.

2  Changes in industry and employment; the growth of light industries, e.g. making electrical goods, and service industries, such as banking, made more opportunities for women. There they could compete on more equal terms.

3  The struggle for votes for women; one reason that some women supported this was that they thought it would lead to more equality in employment.

4  The work of trade unions; in 1888 the match-girls of Bryant & May had formed a union and successfully gone on strike for better conditions. Their example encouraged other unskilled workers to form unions. Trade unions tried to increase their membership of women to struggle for better conditions.

5  The effects of the First World War; attitudes to women changed due to the great part played by women, both at home and abroad. A nurse described the horrors of the battlefield.

**Source 9.16**

*The shells began to scream overhead. In the hospital we found the wounded all yelling like mad things, thinking they were going to be left behind. We sat in the cellars with seventy wounded men to take care of. There was only one line of bricks between us and the shells.*

The Government was in no doubt about the importance of women to the war effort, as this 1916 poster shows.

**Source 9.17**    A poster encouraging women to enrol as munitions workers.

ON HER THEIR LIVES DEPEND

WOMEN MUNITION WORKERS

Enrol at once

The overall picture after the war was far from rosy, as the following source shows.

| Source | 9.18 | An extract from 'The Cause' by R. Strachey, 1928. |

*Thousands upon thousands of women workers were dismissed and found no work to do. It is terribly hard on the women. Everyone assumed that they would quietly go back to their homes, but this was impossible. Because of the war one woman in three had to be self-supporting. Prices were nearly double what they had been in 1914, and the women who had been able to live on their small allowances or fixed incomes could do so no more. Public opinion assumed that all women could still be supported by men, and that if they went on working it was some kind of deliberate wickedness. The very same people who had been heroines and saviours of their country a few months before were now parasites or blacklegs.*

## Activities

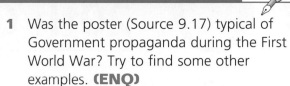

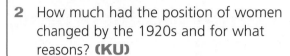

1 Was the poster (Source 9.17) typical of Government propaganda during the First World War? Try to find some other examples. **(ENQ)**

2 How much had the position of women changed by the 1920s and for what reasons? **(KU)**

CREDIT LEVEL

# 10 Transport in the 20th Century

## The railways at their peak, 1880–1914

FOUNDATION/GENERAL LEVEL

**Source 10.1** A drawing of the trains which ran on the Liverpool to Manchester line in the 1830s.

**Source 10.2** A photograph of the train to London as it waits in Central Station, Glasgow in 1910.

In 1900, Britain's railways were at their peak. The London & North Western Railway was the largest joint stock company in the world. Most had earned large profits for years. Some had been passed on to their shareholders, the rest had been put back into the business; bigger locomotives made journeys faster; better carriages made journeys more comfortable; better stations made arrival more pleasant. Some idea of the changes can be seen by comparing the two trains on page 52. The trains in Source 10.1 ran on the Liverpool & Manchester line in the 1830s; the train in Source 10.2, of London & North Western coaches, is pulled by a Caledonian Railway locomotive, built in 1906. It was the most powerful in Britain at that time.

Whilst the companies advertised their facilities widely, they also built hotels like Turnberry, Cruden Bay and Gleneagles (below).

**Source 10.4** The Forth Bridge being built in the late 1880s.

Railways even ran bus services to link up with their own stations. The Great North of Scotland Railway ran this bus between Ballater and Braemar.

**Source 10.3** Gleneagles Hotel, built in 1923.

The railway network in Britain reached its greatest extent at this time. The Firth of Forth was bridged in 1890 while lines were also driven into the highlands.

**Source 10.5** A Milnes-Daimler 16/18hp bus which ran between Ballater and Braemar in 1904.

## Activities

1 Compare the trains from the 1830s (Source 10.1) with the one from the early twentieth century (Source 10.2). What improvements in facilities on trains took place by 1900? **(ENQ)**

2 What attempts did railway companies make to attract more passengers? (Try to find at least four.) **(KU)**

FOUNDATION/GENERAL LEVEL

CREDIT LEVEL

## The railways in difficulties

While in 1900 the railways stood supreme, by 1920 they were almost bankrupt. There were three major reasons for this.

◆ During the First World War the Government took over the railways. The railways were busier than ever before, but repairs were not made as often as they should have been. This happened because workshops had to concentrate on making guns and munitions. When the war ended, many of the railways were in a poor state.

◆ War had also encouraged the development of more efficient ways of manufacturing lorries and cars. For the first time, the railways had to face the competition of another form of transport.

◆ In the years after 1919, many industries found themselves in difficulties as trade and the demand for their goods declined. This included heavy industry such as steel-making and mining – two of the railways' best customers!

To help the railways become more competitive, the Government grouped them into four large companies – the London Midland Scottish, the Southern, the Great Western and the London & North Eastern Railways. This, they hoped, would reduce duplication and waste, and make them better able to withstand the new competition. They were not allowed, however, to adjust their fares, or vary charges between customers. The railways also tried to attract customers by running new, faster trains such as the Royal Scot and the Flying Scotsman.

### Activities

1 Why did the railways have problems after 1919? **(KU)**

2 How helpful was the Government toward the railways, in your opinion. Again, justify your answer. **(KU)**

**Group Activity**

Imagine your group is the Board of Directors of one of the new railway companies in 1923. What plans would you make to try and make your company profitable? Remember that the Government will not give you any money to invest, and banks are not likely to lend you any. (Any group that comes up with more than two ideas deserves a prize!)

## Motor cars and mass production

Before 1914, cars were expensive. They were built to order, and each part was made by hand. No British car maker managed to produce more than one car per year per worker. But lorries and cars were badly needed in France when war broke out, and the British Government sent experts to America to learn how to speed up output.

Henry Ford had built the world's first assembly line near Detroit, to mass produce his Ford Model T. Workers stood beside a moving conveyor belt, and attached a part to the car as it moved past. Ford produced a cheap, basic car, but he made more than one a minute. This system was copied in Britain, to produce cars, lorries and electrical goods such as radios.

F/G LEVEL

Source **10.6**

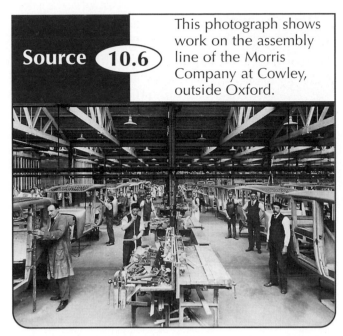

This photograph shows work on the assembly line of the Morris Company at Cowley, outside Oxford.

Working in these new industries was much more pleasant than in older industries. For a start, work was usually indoors; factories were smaller, cleaner and brighter; they were much less dangerous, and often the wages were better. As these industries were growing, there was much less chance of being unemployed.

Mass production methods were common in these new industries. Not everyone liked them, as the following source shows.

Source **10.7**

An extract from Walter Greenwood, 'How the Other Man Lives,' 1939.

*Any man of spirit preferred the dole to the high pay that could be earned. I was not used to mixing with men who put up with so many rules. I found them spineless, money-grabbing and selfish. They didn't care about other workers.*

Until then, Britain had depended on older industries like cotton, coal and shipbuilding. Most of Britain's old industries were in the north of the country. These were the ones worst hit by the Depression in trade after 1929. The south of the country was much less affected, because that was where the new industries like car manufacturing and electrical goods production had grown.

Source **10.8**

Location of old and new industries in Britain in the 1930s.

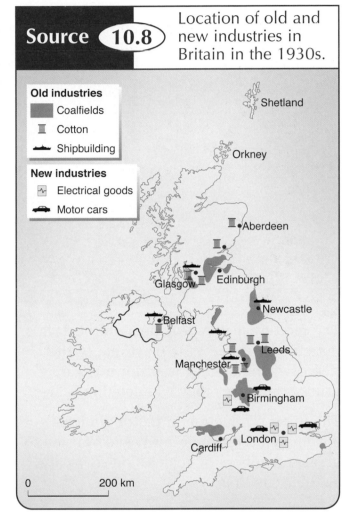

**Old industries**
- Coalfields
- Cotton
- Shipbuilding

**New industries**
- Electrical goods
- Motor cars

Shetland
Orkney
Aberdeen
Glasgow  Edinburgh
Newcastle
Belfast
Leeds
Manchester
Birmingham
Cardiff  London

0        200 km

## Activities

1  Which new industries grew after 1919? **(KU)**

2  In what five ways were conditions better for workers in these industries than in the old industries? **(KU)**

3  Do you agree that the car industry is a mass production industry? Explain your answer. **(KU)**

4  What words show that Greenwood did not like the type of man that worked in the car industry? **(ENQ)**

FOUNDATION/GENERAL LEVEL

CREDIT LEVEL

# The coming of the motor car

Source 10.9

This photograph was taken on the 'Rest and be Thankful' road in Argyll in 1907.

Source 10.10

This photograph was taken on Oxford Street, in central London, in 1922.

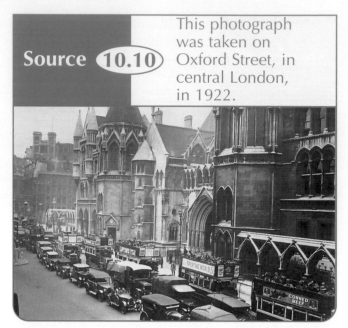

Other types of motor vehicles appeared, as shown by this photograph taken in Edinburgh.

The motor car was developed in the 1880s, but its cost made it the plaything of the rich. Sometimes they went for a leisurely drive; sometimes they competed in rallies.

The mass-production of motor vehicles during and after the First World War led to greater numbers of vehicles on the roads, as their cost fell.

Soon new types of vehicles appeared, some carrying people and others transporting all sorts of goods, as Sources 10.10 and 10.11 show.

Source 10.11

A baker's delivery van.

As more and more people were able to buy cars, changes began to take place in the layout of houses and streets. If you look at Source 10.12 you can see that this middle-class house has lots of room for cars to park.

The space outside this house allows room for vehicles to park.

Soon the government had to introduce ways to control traffic. Roads had to be made safer. The first traffic lights appeared in London in 1926. In 1934 the pedestrian crossing (the 'Belisha Beacon') was introduced. The 30mph speed limit was abolished in 1930, but when road deaths reached 7 000 per year, it was brought back in built-up areas.

## Activities

1  Why did only rich people have motor cars before the First World War? **(KU)**

2  Why did cars become more common after the First World War? **(KU)**

3  What problems arose as more people owned cars? **(KU)**

4  How useful is Source 10.10 as evidence about road transport in Britain in the 1920s? **(KU)**

# The development of town transport

Perhaps the biggest change in this period was the development of transport in urban areas. One of the biggest changes, the growth of motor transport, has already been mentioned.

Source **10.13** Richard Tames discussed the reasons for this growth in 'Railways', 1970.

*The petrol-driven vehicle offered many advantages. It could go almost anywhere. The manufacturer and the shopkeeper with deliveries to make saw obvious advantages in door-to-door service and freedom from the railway timetable. Motor transport was faster over short distances and in towns. It was often cheaper as road haulage companies were free to pick their customers and offer special rates, while the railways were required to charge the same to all users and to run trains in country areas, whether they made a profit or not.*

New vehicles appeared in even greater numbers during the '20s and '30s. Bus services also developed, like that shown in Source 10.14.

The other major change in town transport was the development of the tramcar. The earliest ones were often run by private firms.

Tramcars had several advantages in towns. They could run right through city centre streets, making frequent stops. They could run a frequent service, with only a few minutes between cars. They could move large numbers quickly and were cheap! The journey from Paisley to Airdrie, a distance of 20 miles, cost the princely sum, in 1919, of 1p.

**Source** 10.14   Aberdeen's first motor bus.

## Activities

1   Why were motor vehicles so successful in towns? **(KU)**

2   What advantages did tramcars have over other forms of transport in towns? **(KU)**

# 11 Home and health

## Housing

By 1900 the home life of the upper classes had become very comfortable, as this account by Mrs C. S. Peel tells us.

> **Source 11.1** An extract from 'Life's Enchanted Cup', 1933.

*We modernised it with electric light and a telephone. The house, when rebuilt, contained a large basement, three sitting rooms, a lounge-hall, and seven bedrooms. All the rooms were warmed by coal fires. There were nursery meals to be carried up and down, hot water to the bedrooms ...*

*We had a Norland nurse (nanny), a parlourmaid, a housemaid and a cook. Later we had a manservant for £70 a year. The cook earned £28, the nurse £40. We spent about 12 shillings (60p) each week on food and cleaning materials. We bought coal at 15 shillings (75p) a ton.*

The life of the poor was not so pleasant. A Royal Commission on Housing 1884–5 discovered that drains, water supply, building and sanitation were just as bad in many places as they had been in the 1830s.

## Life in the country

The agricultural depression at the end of the nineteenth century meant farmers could not afford to improve housing for their workers. Often this meant very poor housing and sanitation as this description of a cottage at Eltisley in Cambridgeshire shows.

> **Source 11.2** A passage from H. Rider Haggard's 'Rural England', 1906.

*Two rooms and no outhouse or pantry. I measured the upstairs room. At the floor line it was 17 feet 7 inches by 9 feet but as the room sloped the space above was not so large. The window was 24 inches by 18 inches. In this room eight children were raised with their parents. In the sister cottage adjoining, also two roomed, lived seven children and their parents making a total of nineteen, whose water supply was a filthy hole in the garden. Now water can be fetched from a well some 600 yards away.*

As late as 1939, Dunbarton County Council passed bye-laws to provide minimum living conditions for unmarried farm workers (Source 11.3).

> **Source 11.3**

*Each agricultural worker should have a separate bedstead with a clean mattress and pillow filled with straw ... 2 clean blankets (summer) and 4 the rest of the year.*

*The employer should provide a table with sufficient chairs, a suitable fireplace or stove, lanterns or lamps fixed to the walls to prevent the risk of fire ... sufficient basins or tubs.*

FOUNDATION/GENERAL LEVEL

## Living in the Towns

Housing was no better in towns. Charles Booth reported this about no. 1 Tarleton Street, London in 1900.

**Source 11.4**

From Charles Booth, 'Life and Labour of the London Poor', 1900.

*The ground floor rooms are occupied by Fletcher, a pedlar, his wife and 6 children. He goes round with a barrow, she does washing and charring. On the first floor in front are Lawson, his wife and 2 children; clean and tidy people. In the back room lives Bewley with wife and 4 children. The wife keeps the family by dress making. They also have a niece of 18 living with them.*

*Eight feet square – that is about the average of many of these rooms. Walls and ceilings are black with filth. Sewage is running down the walls. What goes by the name of a window is half of it stuffed with rags to keep out the wind and rain.*

From 1890, Housing Acts encouraged local authorities to get rid of the worst of the slums and to build new cheap housing. Glasgow in 1906 chose the tenement as the type of housing to be built, as shown in Source 11.5.

Life was not always easy for families in the new tenements. Rosalind Elder was born in Glasgow in 1926 and grew up in just such a tenement. Her opinion of tenement life is given in Source 11.6.

**Source 11.6**

*They (the tenements) were horrendous, no 'Wally Close' where we lived. Just dark green paint and whitewash and worn concrete stairs, a shared toilet as well. Must say though that they were clean.*

A 'Wally Close' had tiles on the walls at the entrance to the tenement.

It was not until after 1918 that new council house schemes began to appear all over the country. Many of the homes were semi-detached. They cost around £500 to build and the weekly rent of houses such as those overleaf in York was around 15 shillings 11d (79p) in 1935.

**Source 11.5** Kennyhill Tenements, Glasgow, 1906.

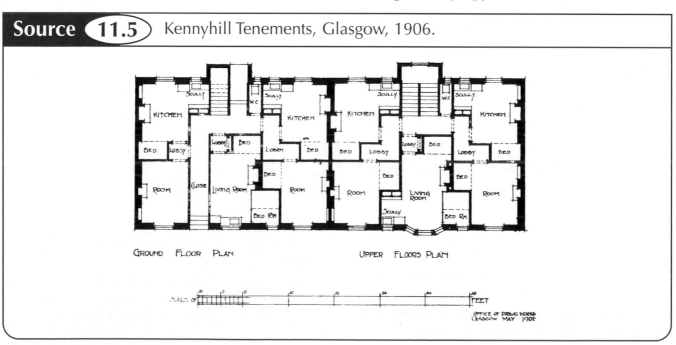

GROUND FLOOR PLAN          UPPER FLOORS PLAN

SCALE OF          FEET

OFFICE OF PUBLIC WORKS
GLASGOW MAY 1906

**Source 11.7**

These council houses in York are typical of the semi-detached houses built after the First World War.

# Health

The poor housing was harming the health of the British people. In 1903, recruitment figures for the army showed that one recruit in three had to be turned away because of poor health.

**Source 11.8**

A Surrey clergyman described his parish in a letter to 'The Times', 5 October 1906.

*... In our country parish there are 2 000 inhabitants. Since January 1st 1906, we had had 27 burials, 12 of which have been children aged two and under. Of the last seven burials, six have been children under 8 months and there are more likely to die. There is no epidemic ... The doctors know most of the children are poorly fed ...*

Reports like these led to the Liberal Government of 1906–14 introducing medical inspections for school children in 1907 and free treatment for needy children from 1912. The National Health Insurance Act of 1911 was extended so that it covered 20 million people by 1938.

Many poor people still could not afford to pay for treatment and had to rely on free treatment in the poor law hospitals. The depression of the 1930s made things worse as a survey of 1936 showed that only 30 per cent of the nation was fed properly and that 10 per cent – 4 500 000 people – were very badly fed. This was worst in areas of high unemployment.

## Activities

1 Give five pieces of evidence from Source 11.1 to show that this family were well-off. **(KU)**

2 What problems were there for a family living in the cottages described in Source 11.2. **(KU)**

3 a) Draw a box 16 cm square and divide it into quarters.

 b) Label the boxes: upstairs, downstairs, front and back.

 c) In each room write the name of the correct family from 1 Tarleton Street.

 d) In each room put a matchstick figure for each person. Make a child half the size of an adult.

4 Look at the letter to 'The Times' newspaper in 1906 again. How valuable is this as evidence about health in the countryside before 1914? **(ENQ)**

5 Look at Sources 11.4 and 11.7. What were the problems facing the Fletcher family? How do you think these problems had been removed by houses such as the council houses built in York? **(KU)**

6 What were the real causes of ill-health in Britain at this time? **(KU)**

**Group Work**
Measure out the size of the rooms in Tarleton Street (Source 11.4).
Pretend to be the people living there.
Each family in turn will move into their house.
Discuss three problems the family will find.

# Housing

At the end of the nineteenth century, suburbs for the middle classes grew up around most towns. The houses were often well-built detached or semi-detached villas and many are still lived in today. Source 11.9 is a plan for one of these Victorian villas, showing the upstairs and downstairs layout of the house. They were comfortable and spacious homes but they were too expensive for working class families to buy.

**Source 11.9**    A Victorian villa plan.

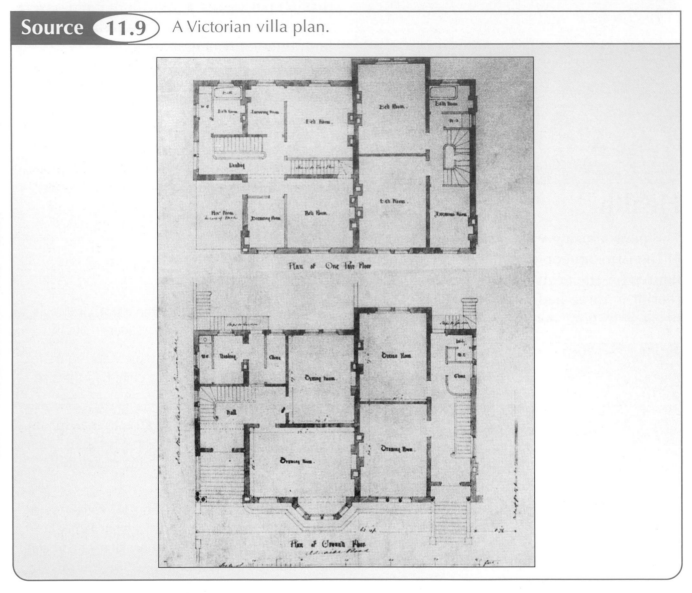

At the end of the nineteenth century, suburbs for the middle classes grew up in most towns. Many of these detached or semi-detached villas can still be seen.

In 1912 the Board of Trade looked into rents being paid by working class families and wrote this as part of its report about housing in Glasgow.

**Source 11.10** Is an extract from the Board of Trade Enquiry into Working-class Rents, 1912.

*The typical house of a working class family is a flat of two or three rooms in a stone-built tenement block, two, three or four stories high. The building is entered by a passage or 'close' leading to a stone stair which goes to the upper floors. Two, three or four flats are found on each floor, and the door by which each flat is entered is on the landing or 'stairhead'. All the rooms in the flat open on to a fair-sized lobby . . . The rooms are large and often had a bed-recess with space for a double bed . . . Some of the family have to sleep in the bed-recess in the living room where the air is more or less polluted. The small number of rooms makes it difficult to separate the sexes in a growing family, or sick children from those who are well and younger children are often disturbed when the older ones go to bed.*

*Usually each block of flats had a common wash-house and drying ground which the families take turns to use. The most obvious disadvantages . . . are shared toilets and the fact most flats are at the head of one or more flights of stairs.*

*On the other hand, the tenement has several distinct advantages. It is, as a rule, exceptionally well-built with large high rooms and the workman can live near his work and avoid travelling expenses.*

Between the wars, governments had three main aims in housing: to get rid of slums, build more and better houses and see working people charged rents they could afford. However, actual building was slow until the Addison Act of 1921 allowed local authorities to build 210 000 houses before grants were cut. Chamberlain's Act of 1923 gave grants to private builders who built 440 000 houses by 1929. Unfortunately, these were too expensive for the people who really needed them. The Wheatley Act of 1924 gave grants to local councils who built 500 000 houses by 1933. However, this did not solve the problems of slums and although Greenwood's Act of 1930 gave council grants to clear slums and rehouse tenants, resulting in 250 000 slum houses being cleared by 1939, the truth was that more than half a million slum houses still remained.

# Health and housing since the 1870s

Government investigations showed the relationship between overcrowding and ill-health. In 1871, 32.5 per cent of all Scottish houses had only one room and 37.6 per cent had only two rooms. By 1911 only 12.8 per cent were single rooms and 40.4 per cent were two-roomed houses. The census also showed that in 1911 56 per cent of the single rooms had more than two people living in them. Medical officers of health reported that in houses of one room, 32 per cent of children died before reaching the age of five but that the rate dropped to 2 per cent in houses of five or more rooms.

From the 1870s onwards, housing, diet and medical improvements reduced health risks to babies, as the following table shows. The table shows how many babies out of each thousand born died before their first birthday. This is called the Infant Mortality Rate.

Government concern about these figures was shown when more than 3500 welfare clinics for infants and nearly 1800 ante-natal clinics were opened between 1918 and 1938.

**Source 11.11** Infant Mortality Rate for Glasgow and Scotland.

| Year | Glasgow | Scotland |
|------|---------|----------|
| 1871 | 191 | 130 |
| 1881 | 144 | 113 |
| 1891 | 148 | 128 |
| 1901 | 149 | 129 |
| 1911 | 139 | 113 |
| 1921 | 106 | 90 |
| 1931 | 105 | 82 |
| 1941 | 111 | 83 |

## Activities

1  Study Sources 11.1 and 11.9.
   In what ways were middle and upper class houses comfortable to live in? **(KU)**

2  How far did governments between the First and Second World Wars succeed in their three aims as regards housing? **(KU)**

3  Use any of the sources to explain what were the most important causes of ill-health in Britain in the period 1880–1939? **(KU)**

4  Why was the infant mortality rate for Glasgow higher than the Scottish average? **(KU)**

5  How useful is Source 11.10 as evidence about housing before 1914? **(ENQ)**

# 12 Votes for women

At the beginning of the nineteenth century, women had very few rights. Even rich girls had little education as men thought that their place was in the home. A wife was seen as her husband's property and he controlled her. Some laws had been passed to help women but many were still badly treated in 1898 as Mrs Pankhurst, who fought for votes for women, explains. Look at the table on page 68 to see some of these changes.

| Source 12.1 | From Emmeline Pankhurst, 'My Own Story', 1914. |
|---|---|

*As registrar of births and deaths in a working class district . . . the women used to tell me their stories, dreadful stories some of them. I was shocked to be reminded over and over again how little respect there was in the world for women and children.*

*. . . As a member of the school board I soon found that men teachers received much higher wages, although many of the women had to teach sewing and domestic science in addition to their regular class work. They received no extra pay and often spent part of their poor salaries to provide dinners for very poor children.*

*. . . Manchester Technical College girls were kept out of bakery because the men's trade unions objected to their being educated for such skilled work. It was clear men regarded women as a servant class.*

Women had been trying to get parliament to give them the vote since 1867 but despite thousands of meetings and petitions with millions of signatures, the peaceful **suffragist** societies were getting nowhere. In 1903 Mrs Pankhurst started the WSPU (Women's Social and Political Union) whose motto was 'Deeds not words'. In the 1905 election campaign they went to meetings to ask MPs if they would give women the vote. This is what happened when Annie Kenney asked this at the Manchester Free Trade Hall.

| Source 12.2 | A second extract from Emmeline Pankhurst, 'My Own Story'. |
|---|---|

*The audience became a mob. They howled, they shouted and roared, shaking their fists fiercely at the woman who dared to ask her question at a man's meeting. Hands were lifted to drag her out of her chair but Christabel . . . helped ward off the mob, who struck and scratched at her until her sleeve was red with blood.*

Stewards threw the women out while the Liberal leaders sat and did nothing. Outside, the women spoke to the crowds and Annie and Christabel Pankhurst (Mrs Pankhurst's daughter), were arrested. They refused to pay a fine and went to jail. This received lots of publicity and forced men to start taking them seriously.

Women continued to explain why they should receive the vote, as Source 12.3 shows.

**FOUNDATION/GENERAL LEVEL**

**Source** 12.3  A suffragette poster from around 1910.

Only by becoming more and more militant were women able to get attention for their views, and marches on Parliament became fairly common. These women were the **suffragettes**.

On 2 July 1909, Marion Wallace Dunlop went on hunger strike because she was treated like an ordinary criminal. After 91 hours without food she was released. Naturally, other suffragettes did the same.

In September, the Home Secretary ordered force feeding. Mary Leigh was one of the first to suffer. She describes what happened in Source 12.4.

The Government argued they had to feed the women as they could not let them die or release them to commit more crime. Many people were horrified at the cruelty of the Government.

After a general election which showed the Liberals had lost a lot of support, there was a rest from the action as it looked as if the Government might grant reform. When the Government changed their minds the violence started again.

From March 1912 a campaign of the destruction of property began with the

**Source** 12.4

*The wardresses forced me on to the bed and the 2 doctors came in with them. While I was held down a nasal tube was inserted. It is two metres long with a funnel at the end. The end is put up one nostril ... Great pain is felt. The drums of the ear seem to be bursting, a horrible pain in the throat and breast. The tube is pushed down 20 inches (50 cms) ... Then the other doctor, who is behind, forces the other end up the nostrils ... The one holding the funnel end pours the liquid down, about a pint of milk, sometimes egg and milk are used ... I was very sick on the first occasion after the tube was withdrawn.*

breaking of windows in the West End of London. Pillar boxes were set on fire, Ayr racecourse and buildings in Edinburgh, Aberdeen, Dundee and elsewhere were set on fire between 1913 and 1914.

**Source** 12.5  The Suffragette view of the Temporary Discharge Act 1913.

On 4 June 1913, Emily Wilding Davison was killed when she threw herself in front of the King's horse during the Derby race. She thought men might take women more seriously if they showed they were willing to die for their cause.

The Government did not want martyrs and in 1913 they passed the Prisoners' Temporary Discharge for Ill-Health Act which let them release hunger-strikers from prison and then re-arrest them when they were healthy again. A typical suffragette view of this Act is shown in Source 12.5.

# The First World War

When war broke out with Germany in 1914, the women stopped the violence. Emmeline and Christabel Pankhurst encouraged men to enlist and women to work in the factories. Over 70 000 women volunteered their services to the Government. After conscription was introduced, many more women were needed to take over men's jobs. The following table shows just how many more women were needed in different jobs.

| Source 12.6 | The increase in women workers between 1914 and 1918. |
|---|---|
| Engineering industry | Up 800 000 |
| Munitions (arms) factories | Up 606 000 |
| Government departments | Up 200 000 |
| Clerical work in offices | Up 500 000 |
| On the land (farm workers) | Up 250 000 |
| Women's Services | Up 100 000 |
| Nurses | Up 100 000 |
| YMCA | Up 30 000 |

Women did not only serve at home. Source 12.7 shows that they also drove ambulances in France.

Their help in winning the war led to some

women over 30 gaining the vote in 1918 and all women over 21 gaining it in 1928.

Source 12.7 Baroness T'Serclaes and Mairi Chisholm with their ambulance at the French Front.

## Activities

1 For what reasons did women want the vote? (Sources 12.1 and 12.3) **(KU)**

2 How did some men react when women demanded the vote? (Account and Source 12.2) **(KU)**

3 Use the headings below and draw a table showing women's struggle for the vote and how the Government reacted to their methods. (The first and last ones have been done for you.)

| Date | Methods of Women | Government Reaction |
|---|---|---|
| 1867–1903 | meetings, petitions | ignore |
| 1914–18 | war work | vote to some women |

4 Why were women over 30 given the right to vote in 1918? **(KU)**

5 Choose one of the posters (Sources 12.3 or 12.5).

   a) What is it trying to say?

   b) How effective do you think it is? Explain your answer. **(KU)**

# Women's rights

This table shows the laws passed and other changes in the nineteenth century to improve women's conditions.

## Source 12.8

| Date | Law Passed |
| --- | --- |
| 1834 | Women were allowed to vote in town council elections. |
| 1848 | Queen's College for Women opened to give women an education equal to men. |
| 1857 | If her husband deserted her, a woman could keep her own wages. |
| 1860 | The Nightingale School for Nurses was opened. |
| 1870 | Women could vote for the New School Boards. |
| 1873 | Girton, the first women's college, opened at Cambridge University. |
| 1876 | Medical Schools were allowed to take women students. |
| 1880 | Women could vote in county council elections. |
| 1880 | Married women could keep their own property. |
| 1886 | If the father died, a woman could become the legal parent of her children. |
| 1886 | A husband who deserted his wife had to pay her maintenance. |
| 1891 | A husband could not imprison his wife. |

## Source 12.9

Peaceful Groups like the National Union of Women's Suffragist Societies (NUWSS) set out arguments for and against votes for women.

B. 60.

**National Union of Women's Suffrage Societies,**
14, GT. SMITH STREET, WESTMINSTER, LONDON, S.W.
LAW-ABIDING.                         NON-PARTY.

President :—Mrs. HENRY FAWCETT, LL.D.
Colours—Red, White and Green.

# Anti-Suffrage Arguments.

Anti-Suffragists say that the "The Voter, in giving a vote, pledges himself to uphold the consequences of his vote at all costs" and that "women are physically incapable of making this pledge."

### What does this Mean?

When the issue at a General Election is PEACE or WAR, and a man votes for WAR, does he himself have to fight?

### No ! !

The men who fight are seldom qualified to vote, and the men who vote are never compelled to fight.

### What is the Voters part in War?

He is called upon to PAY THE BILL.

### Are Women Physically incapable of this?

Apparently **NOT.**

They are forced to pay in equal proportions with the men who alone have made the decision. Surely this is not fair! Since men and women are equally involved in the consequences, should not men and women equally have power to decide?

"But some matters discussed in the House of Commons concern men more than women."

True, but just as many concern women more than men.

Is not the Housing Problem a woman's question since

### "Woman's Place is the Home?"

Are not EDUCATION, a Pure Milk Supply, and a Children's Charter questions for women, since

### "The Woman's Business is to look after the Baby?"

Is not the Taxation of Food a woman's question since women are

### "The Housekeepers of the Nation?"

Women claim **votes**, not because they are, or want to be, LIKE MEN, but because they are **Different**, and have somewhat different interests and different views. They want the vote as a tool, with which to do **not Men's Work**, but **Women's Work,** which men have left undone, or are trying unsuccessfully to do.

# LET THE WOMEN HELP !

### "Two Heads are Better than one!!"

Published by the NATIONAL UNION OF WOMEN'S SUFFRAGE SOCIETIES,
14, Great Smith Street, S.W.: and
Printed by THE TEMPLAR PRINTING WORKS, 198, Edmund Street, Birmingham.

The Women's Social Political Union used stronger methods, campaigning against the Liberal Government of 1905–14. After Asquith, who was against women's suffrage, became Prime Minister in 1908, their chances seemed poor, as seen by Mrs Pankhurst's account of Home Secretary, Herbert Gladstone's speech.

**Source 12.10** From 'My Own Story' by Emmeline Pankhurst.

*First academic discussion, then effective action, was the history of men's suffrage. (Men) know the necessity of demonstrating the greatness of their movement . . . they assembled in their tens of thousands all over the country. Of course, it is not to be expected that women can assemble in such masses, but power belongs to the masses, and through this power a government can be influenced . . .*

The women retaliated on 21 June 1907 with a march of 200 000 in Hyde Park. Asquith refused to change his mind and would not meet a deputation of women on 30 June. Police stopped the women marching on Parliament.

## The government's view

Some of the Liberal Ministers, like Lloyd-George and Winston Churchill, were sympathetic to the women's cause but others were against them. The Government had many other problems at home and abroad which demanded their attention. They were also afraid that if they gave women householders the vote, these middle class women would vote Conservative, so making it harder for the Liberals to win

elections. They therefore delayed a decision.

Then, when the violence was stepped up from 1910, the Government was determined not to give in to force in case it encouraged other groups. The country was divided over the question of the vote for women and they knew whatever they did would make them unpopular.

### Activities

1  a) In what ways were women second class citizens in the early nineteenth century? **(KU)**

   b) What political rights did they gain before 1900? **(KU)**

   c) Use Sources 12.1, 12.3 and 12.6 to explain why they claimed the right to vote. **(KU)**

   d) Do you think Source 12.3 or 12.5 is the more effective piece of propaganda? Explain your answer. **(ENQ)**

2  Describe the methods used by the WSPU. **(KU)**

3  How far do Source 12.10 and the actions of the Government justify the militant action of the WSPU? **(KU)**

# 13 Enquiry skills: Investigating

At General and Credit levels you are expected to show that you can use enquiry skills to investigate a question, an issue, a proposition (suggestion) or an hypothesis (theory). You will work with historical evidence and reach a conclusion based on what you find **and** on other evidence you have gathered elsewhere in your studies.

The first task you will have is to make judgements about some of the evidence you are offered for your investigation. For example, this means writing about the kinds of source evidence you are looking at **and** who produced the sources in the first place. You can say whether the evidence is primary or secondary **and** something about who produced it **or** when it was produced **or** why it was produced. You can also write about the amount of relevant information in the sources **or** even compare what is in one source with what is in another. **Or** you might want to write about the accuracy of the source evidence or examples of bias in it.

Your next task will be to record relevant evidence from the sources which will help with your investigation. This evidence may **either** support **or** not support the ideas or views in the question or hypothesis you are investigating. Try to set out the evidence you gather clearly in notes which will be understandable to someone else even if you are not there to explain what you mean.

Doing these two tasks will prepare you for the final one – writing your conclusion to the investigation. Remember **three** important things about this conclusion:

◆ you must express your own opinion(s) clearly;

◆ your opinion must be supported by relevant evidence;

◆ you must try to add at least one other piece of evidence you know of and which is not from one of the sources you have been given.

It is very likely, especially at Credit level, that you will want to write about evidence for **and** against the view or theory you are investigating before giving your own opinion. This means you are balancing the evidence in order to reach a more convincing and balanced conclusion.

Here is an example of the kind of investigation you should be able to complete.

**The issue to investigate is:**

*Working class housing in Scotland improved greatly between 1917 and 1939.*

**Study the sources carefully and answer the questions which follow. You should use your own knowledge where appropriate**.

Source A is part of a Royal Commission report on 'Working Class Housing in Scotland' which was published in 1917.

## Source  A

*Houses and villages are in unsatisfactory places. There are insufficient supplies of water and unsatisfactory drainage. There is a very inadequate provision for the removal of refuse and widespread evidence of decent sanitary conveniences. In many mining areas there are still unspeakably filthy privy-middens and on farms there are badly built, damp labourers' cottages. There is great overcrowding in the big industrial towns, with large families in one-room homes.*

Source B is a photograph of a new, timber house in Motherwell visited by the King and Queen in 1938.

| Source B | **Timber house**, Watling St, Motherwell. |
|---|---|

Source C is from *50 Special Years. A Study in Scottish Housing* by Tom Begg, published in 1987.

## Source  C

*In 1935 18 814 council houses were completed in Scotland. By the end of 1938 almost all of the slum houses identified in 1934 had been cleared and 40 000 replacement houses had been built. A lot less progress had been made with the continuing problem of overcrowding. One-quarter of new council houses had only two rooms.*

GENERAL/CREDIT LEVEL

# General and Credit levels: questions you may be asked.

**Question 1**. How useful are Sources A and B for investigating changes in working class housing between 1917 and 1939?

Remember usefulness/value of evidence such as these sources depends upon things such as:

◆ who wrote, drew or photographed the evidence,

◆ when the evidence was produced,

◆ why the evidence was produced,

◆ whether or not it seems to you that the evidence has been exaggerated or organised to make it support a particular point of view, as in a cartoon for instance,

◆ does the evidence agree/disagree with other evidence you have seen,

◆ how much relevant evidence the source contains – e.g. a little, a lot, some.

**DO NOT** write out all the relevant evidence in Source A, for example **OR** explain everything you can see in the photograph which is Source B. This is not only a waste of your time but shows you do not really know how to evaluate evidence.

At Credit level you should be thinking about balancing strengths and weaknesses you are able to identify in the sources in your answer.

**Question 2**. What evidence is there in the sources about problems in housing between 1917 and 1939? What evidence in the sources suggests housing was improving?

This time you **SHOULD** write down the evidence you find in the sources – for example about problems you should write that from Source A you learn that:

◆ many houses did not have good water supplies or good drains,

◆ often rubbish was not removed,

◆ in the houses there was overcrowding,

From Source B you see evidence of improvements such as:

◆ well-built housing in places like Motherwell,

◆ houses with lots of windows to give light and air,

◆ gardens around houses.

And from Source C you learn that:

◆ many slums had been cleared,

◆ many council houses built,

◆ BUT there was still overcrowding in some places.

## THREE IMPORTANT THINGS TO REMEMBER FOR THIS QUESTION

1   If there are 6 marks for the question give at least six pieces of evidence BUT do not waste time trying to give all the evidence you see in the sources.

2   Make sure you use evidence relevant to BOTH parts of the question.

3   Try to use your own words in your answer, this shows you understand the evidence.

**Question 3**. Did working class housing improve greatly between 1917 and 1939? You should use evidence from the sources AND your own knowledge to suggest a conclusion.

Make sure you give a conclusion in your answer – that is say something like;

**I think working class housing improved a little/a lot between 1917 and 1939 because Source A shows how bad it was in 1917 but Source B shows much better houses were being built for people by 1938 and Source C says many slums had been cleared by 1939 and lots of new council houses had been built. I know that after the First World War the government tried to make sure better houses were built for working people and rents were fairer. [RECALL]**

At CREDIT level you should really be trying to make sure you balance your conclusion. So in this case your answer could be:

**I think there was a lot of improvement in working class housing between 1917 and 1939 because Source A gives evidence of very bad conditions in 1917 and the other sources give evidence of improvements, but some problems did remain. For example, according to Source C, there was still overcrowding in some homes, perhaps because new council houses were often small. On the other hand there were many more new council homes and many slums had been cleared. Houses like the one in Source B were**

**better built than older homes. I also know that government acts in the 1920s gave money to private builders and local councils to improve housing. [RECALL].**

1. How useful are Sources A and B for investigating housing in Scotland between 1917 and 1939? Make sure you write about both sources. You can say that both are primary sources, but you must add that what makes them useful is that one was published at the start of the period and the other at the end, giving a range of evidence. You can compare the amount of evidence in the sources, but do not simply write down what they contain. You can write about the authorship of the sources and why this might make them useful.

   *4 marks*

2. What evidence is there in the sources about problems in housing?

   What evidence in the sources suggests that housing was improving?

   *6 marks*

3. Did working class housing improve greatly between 1917 and 1939? You should use evidence from the sources and your own knowledge to reach a balanced conclusion.

   *5 marks*

   (N.B. If you simply agree/disagree or if you only use evidence from these sources you will be given no marks or only some of the marks for this question.)

# 14

# Britain after the Second World War

FOUNDATION/GENERAL LEVEL

By Christmas 1945 the people of Britain had come through a terrible war lasting more than 5 years. Around 400 000 British people were killed in the war and half-a-million homes were destroyed. The war had also created many other problems which needed to be solved after 1945.

## The economy

Britain was deeply in debt, the war having cost £1 million a day in 1939, rising to £16 million daily by 1945. The country owed £35 000 million for war goods bought on credit.

It was important to return to a peacetime economy and produce goods to sell abroad so that the debt could be paid off. However, coal production had dropped from 227 million tonnes in 1939 to 182 million tonnes in 1945 and the railways were overworked and needed huge sums spent on repairs. British trade and influence had been declining since the end of the First World War: how could the country recover when it had lost one-third of its merchant ships and exports were down 60 per cent from 1939?

## Society

People faced hardship as many foods were rationed. Certain foods such as bananas, oranges and ice cream had been unavailable since the start of the war. Clothes were rationed and coal was in short supply.

There was a shortage of 1.25 million houses and returning ex-servicemen needed jobs.

During the war, the Government had begun plans for peacetime, with the Beveridge Report of 1942 leading the way in dealing with poverty. Beveridge planned to give people 'social security' from the 'cradle to the grave'. The Labour Government of 1945–51 carried out the proposals and set up the Welfare State. You will find more information on the Welfare State in Chapter 17 under the heading 'Health'.

## Activities

**1** a) In what two ways had the Second World War put Britain in debt? **(KU)**

   b) Why was it difficult to make goods in Britain to sell abroad? (Give three reasons.) **(KU)**

**2** Give three ways life was hard for people at the end of the war. **(KU)**

**3** Look at Source 14.1 and make up a table showing how the Government intended to tackle the five aspects of poverty. Leave four or five lines between each aspect. (As you work through the following chapters, you can come back and fill in reforms.) **(KU)**

**Source 14.1** How the Government attempted to tackle the five aspects of poverty: disease, squalor, want, ignorance and idleness.

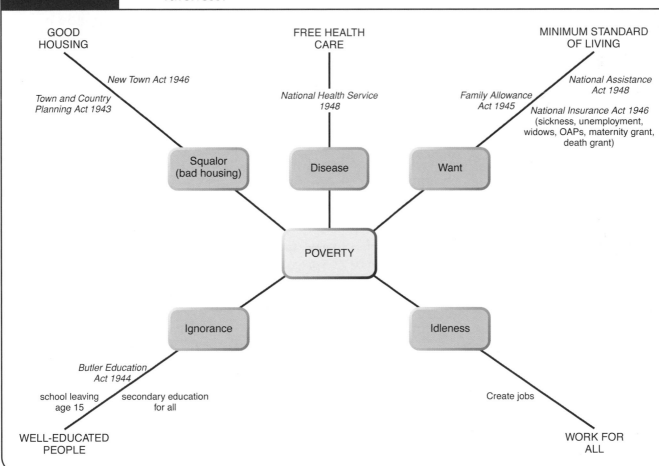

GOOD HOUSING

New Town Act 1946

Town and Country Planning Act 1943

FREE HEALTH CARE

National Health Service 1948

MINIMUM STANDARD OF LIVING

National Assistance Act 1948

Family Allowance Act 1945

National Insurance Act 1946 (sickness, unemployment, widows, OAPs, maternity grant, death grant)

Squalor (bad housing)

Disease

Want

POVERTY

Ignorance

Idleness

Butler Education Act 1944

school leaving age 15

secondary education for all

Create jobs

WELL-EDUCATED PEOPLE

WORK FOR ALL

FOUNDATION/GENERAL LEVEL

CREDIT LEVEL

# Population

Apart from a baby boom just after the war, the birth rate in Britain has remained low as people have chosen to limit the size of their family. At the same time, people are living longer, with the life expectancy in 1978 being 69 for men (46 in 1900) and 76 for women (52 in 1900).

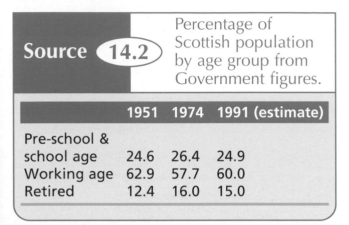

| **Source 14.2** | Percentage of Scottish population by age group from Government figures. | | |
|---|---|---|---|
| | **1951** | **1974** | **1991 (estimate)** |
| Pre-school & school age | 24.6 | 26.4 | 24.9 |
| Working age | 62.9 | 57.7 | 60.0 |
| Retired | 12.4 | 16.0 | 15.0 |

Since the war, governments have been concerned about the distribution of population. Britain averages around 770 people to the square mile with more than 80 per cent of the population living in urban areas. Concern about overcrowding and poor housing in our inner cities has led to the building of carefully planned New Towns.

In Scotland New Towns like East Kilbride, Livingston and Cumbernauld were built between Glasgow and Edinburgh. The New Towns were planned to provide better housing and living conditions than in overcrowded cities. To achieve these aims most houses were of semi-detached two storey construction rather than multi-storey blocks of flats. Many of the people who moved into the New Towns found difficulty adjusting to their new surroundings missed the companionship they had enjoyed in their tenements, the corner shops, the bars, theatres and cinemas which were so accessible in towns but were missing in the New Towns. Only as public transport has improved, car ownership increased and house prices risen greatly in city centres have the New Towns really become very popular. You can find out more about New Towns in Chapter 17.

Improved transport links have made it possible for people to commute considerable distances to work.

## Immigation

In the years after the Second World War most of those coming to Britain came from the West Indies and Africa, and later from India. There were worries that immigrants were taking jobs from the native British population but it seems that this was not the case. The new immigrants tended to move into jobs left by British workers who had moved on to employment with better pay and higher status. In other words, they took on jobs that British workers did not want to do. In cities like London, Leicester and Glasgow immigrants formed their own communities, which led to problems over matters like housing and education and, in places, to some conflicts with the native population.

## Source 14.3 New Towns built in Britain since 1946.

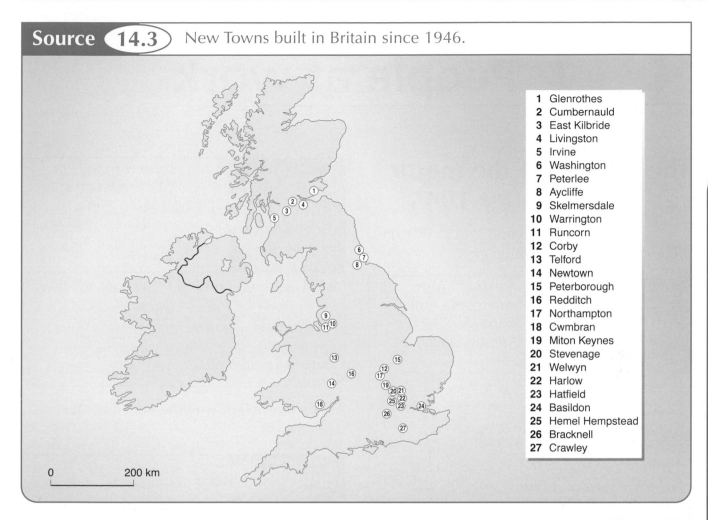

| | |
|---|---|
| 1 | Glenrothes |
| 2 | Cumbernauld |
| 3 | East Kilbride |
| 4 | Livingston |
| 5 | Irvine |
| 6 | Washington |
| 7 | Peterlee |
| 8 | Aycliffe |
| 9 | Skelmersdale |
| 10 | Warrington |
| 11 | Runcorn |
| 12 | Corby |
| 13 | Telford |
| 14 | Newtown |
| 15 | Peterborough |
| 16 | Redditch |
| 17 | Northampton |
| 18 | Cwmbran |
| 19 | Miton Keynes |
| 20 | Stevenage |
| 21 | Welwyn |
| 22 | Harlow |
| 23 | Hatfield |
| 24 | Basildon |
| 25 | Hemel Hempstead |
| 26 | Bracknell |
| 27 | Crawley |

0    200 km

CREDIT LEVEL

## Activities

1 a) What economic problems faced Britain at the end of the Second World War? **(KU)**

   b) Why did she find it difficult to export goods? **(KU)**

2 Write a paragraph about the hardships faced by a returning soldier. **(KU)**

3 a) What five aspects contributing to poverty were identified in the Beveridge Report? **(KU)**

   b) What plans had the Government made to deal with them by 1948? **(KU)**

4 Use sources 14.1 and 14.2 to answer the following:

   a) What changes have taken place in the balance of population since 1951? **(KU)**

   b) What services in the Welfare State would need more money spent on them as a result of these population changes?

5 Use a map of Britain to find out which cities would provide the population for the following New Towns. **(KU)**

| New Town | City |
|---|---|
| East Kilbride | |
| Livingston | |
| Aycliffe | |
| Warrington | |
| Cwmbran | |
| Basildon | |

# 15 People at work

## The growth of the motor car industry after 1945

The outbreak of the Second World War had a big effect on the car industry.

> **Source 15.1** An extract from Pagnamenta and Overy, 'All Our Working Days', 1984.
>
> *When World War Two started, car making stopped. The entire industry was put on to war work. The Castle Bromwich car factory alone provided seven out of each ten Spitfires made. The car makers' knowledge of mass production methods helped build aircraft at a speed the aircraft firms would never have been capable of.*

In wartime, the Government saw the advantages of mass production, just as businessmen had done before it; a large number of goods, of the same size, design, colour and quality could be produced cheaply and quickly; machinery could be used to turn out parts; workers specialised in one task only, which they could do quickly, and which earned them good wages. In 1914 Britain produced 34 000 cars; by 1930, output was 180 000. The cost of a Morris Cowley was £390; a much better model of the same car in 1930 cost £162.

Working conditions were not always pleasant or easy as Sources 15.2 and 15.3 show.

> **Source 15.2** Hayden Evans left Wales to work in a car factory in Oxford. Quoted in Pagnamenta and Overy.
>
> *It was very frightening to start with. I had never been in a place where there was so much noise. The machine I was on was the equivalent of one of those hydraulic picks that they used to dig up the road.*

Another problem was the speed of the assembly line.

> **Source 15.3** Tom Ward remembers.
>
> *You had only so much time to do a job. If you were on ordinary time you got £2, and then you would have to go quicker and quicker to get more. And it would go up to time and a half, £3 a week. And when it got to double time they'd stop, no more, no faster. We could make about £5 a week. It was always good money in the motor trade if you could do the job.*

Stan Campbell, an inspector at the Cowley factory explained what happened to some workers.

> **Source 15.4** A further extract from Pagnamenta and Overy.
>
> *Anyone who couldn't keep up with the job just disappeared, finished up by labouring.*

Perhaps the worst thing about the car industry was being laid off. Sometimes this happened because of production problems, like shortages of parts or breakdowns in the assembly line. More and more often these happened because of strikes over wages or working conditions.

By the end of the 1960s, the British car industry had a dreadful reputation for high prices, poor quality and late delivery. As a result of these problems, more people bought foreign cars. Some were made abroad, but a new development was that foreign makers, especially the Japanese, started up factories of their own in Britain. One example is the Nissan factory near Newcastle. These use mass production methods but output and quality are high. Disputes are almost unknown.

For British makers, the result has been a drop in output, redundancies and the closure of factories. Only in the 1980s, after the industry nearly collapsed, were the newest methods introduced.

Source 15.5

This photograph shows computer controlled robots making Metros at Longbridge. Each of these robot lines replaced 70 car workers.

## Activities

1 Describe work in a car factory using mass production methods. How did mass production methods help Britain's war effort? **(KU)**

2 Why are Hayden Evans and Tom Ward (Sources 15.2 and 15.3) good sources for finding out what it was like to work in the car industry? **(ENQ)**

3 In what ways has the industry changed since 1945? **(KU)**

**Group Activities**
Discuss with a partner the advantages and disadvantages of mass production methods. Make a list for each category.

CREDIT LEVEL

# The car industry in difficulties

There have been many explanations of why the British car industry ran into difficulties. There is no doubt that productivity (output per worker) was a major failing.

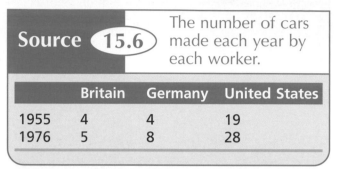

Source **15.6**   The number of cars made each year by each worker.

|      | Britain | Germany | United States |
|------|---------|---------|---------------|
| 1955 | 4       | 4       | 19            |
| 1976 | 5       | 8       | 28            |

Another problem was labour relations. Although order books were full, British companies had made little profit; not enough of the money made had been put back into new plants. Models of cars that should have been replaced were allowed to carry on being produced. This made them less attractive to buyers abroad, and expensive.

By 1974 the situation was so serious that the Government 'think tank', the Central Policy Review Staff, was called in to examine the problem. It explained difficulties in the car industry as follows.

Source **15.7**   From the Central Policy Review.

*There is not the slightest chance of the British car industry becoming profitable at any level of production if the present interruptions to production, reluctance to accept new methods of production and capital equipment, and readiness to accept sub-standard quality continue. These problems reflect the attitudes of management and labour towards each other, towards productivity and towards work.*

Government policies did not always help. They tried to force car firms opening new factories to build them in areas where unemployment was high, such as Merseyside or Central Scotland.

The factories set up this way were not, on the whole, successful. The Linwood plant near Paisley closed after 20 years.

A series of mergers resulted in only four British car producers. A new tough style of management imposed new working practices and slashed the number of models; ten factories were closed and 70 000 jobs lost. Even so, British Leyland lost over £1 300 million in five years. Government money was required to keep the industry alive. It survived and was returned to private hands under the privatisation programme of the Thatcher Government of the 1980s.

Source **15.8**   The Linwood plant after closure. An auction of its machines is in progress.

## Activities

1 What were the reasons for difficulties in the British car industry? **(KU)**

2 How valuable is Source 15.7 as evidence of problems in the car industry? **(ENQ)**

**Group Activities**

Get into groups of three.

a) Make a list of three important reasons for the problems of the car industry.

b) Each take one of these roles:

Management
Workers
Government

Discuss which of you is most responsible for the difficulties of the industry.

# Women at work since 1945

During the Second World War (1939–45), women played an even greater part than they had done in the First World War. As well as taking the places in industry of men who had gone off to fight, the women in the armed services performed well. A US War Department booklet of 1942 put it as follows:

**Source 15.9**

*British women officers often give orders to men. The men obey smartly and know it is no shame. For British women have proved themselves in this war. They have stuck to their posts near burning ammunition dumps, delivered messages on foot after their motorcycles have been blasted from under them.*

The war gave many women the chance to learn skills and trades they could only have dreamt about before. They even became fitters and welders in shipyards, working on equal terms with men, though they were paid less. Even so, many women enjoyed the independence their jobs gave them.

Many also remembered how the advances made during the First World War had been lost when peace returned. They were determined that these gains would not be lost again.

But even after 25 years of campaigning, some women were disappointed with what they had achieved.

**Source 15.10** This article appeared in the 'Shrew' magazine in 1971.

*Women in our society are oppressed. In jobs we do full work for half pay, in the home we do unpaid work fulltime. Legally we often have only the status of children. We are brought up to feel inadequate, educated to narrower horizons than men.*

Changes in industry had helped to create more jobs open to women. The growth of light industries, such as electronics, and service industries, such as banking, recruited large numbers of women. In some cases employers preferred women because of the neatness of their work.

**Source 15.11** Woman working on a production line

But women were still more at the mercy of changes in the economy than men.

**Source 15.12** From F. Wheen, 'The Sixties', 1982.

*A growing number of women had gone out to work during the 1960s; by the late 1970s, with unemployment figures climbing upwards, they were encouraged to give up their jobs. As one of Mrs Thatcher's ministers, Patrick Jenkin, said in 1979: 'If the Good Lord had intended us all having equal rights to go out to work, He wouldn't have created man and woman'.*

## Activities

1  Read Source 15.9. What shows that the US War Department thought British women had performed well during the war? **(KU)**

2  In what ways did women benefit from changes in industry after 1945? **(KU)**

3  What reasons does Source 15.10 give for women's lack of equality? **(KU)**

4  Does any other evidence in the sources support this view? **(ENQ)**

# Women: action against inequality

As a result of pressure by women's groups, governments in the 1960s and '70s passed a series of acts to improve the position of women. The most important of these were:

◆ 1970 Equal Pay Act: men and women should be paid the same wage for doing the same work. [It came into force in 1975.]

◆ 1975 Sex Discrimination Act: women were to get the same treatment as men, by law, in education, training, housing and employment.

It was hoped that these laws would change the inequality in earnings that women suffered in 1975.

**Source 15.13**

| | Average earnings per week | |
| | Manual | Non-Manual |
| --- | --- | --- |
| Men | £55.70 | £68.40 |
| Women | £31.10 | £39.60 |

In 1986, however, Maggy Meade-King, writing in *The Guardian*, commented on the earnings of men and women.

F/G LEVEL

CREDIT LEVEL

CREDIT LEVEL

## Source 15.14

*The latest New Earnings Survey figures for April, 1986, confirm adult male weekly earnings standing at £207 and women's at £137. In YTS, girls are overwhelmingly grouped in clerical work and the retail and caring services. The implications of this are profound. The pay differential between men and women is perpetuated, as are young men's increased opportunities for further training and promotion.*

The Equal Opportunities Commission (EOC) confirmed, the previous year, that women occupied only a fraction of the 'top' jobs.

## Source 15.15

|                      | Male    | Female |
|----------------------|---------|--------|
| Judges, lawyers      | 45 000  | 8 000  |
| Doctors              | 60 000  | 19 000 |
| Accountants          | 204 000 | 23 000 |
| Scientists, engineers| 896 000 | 87 000 |
| Lecturers            | 84 000  | 30 000 |

Even in the House of Commons, which passed the Equal Opportunities Act, only 41 women MPs (6.3 per cent) were elected in 1987.

Women still face yet another handicap in the struggle for equality. Madeleine Jones, in 1989, wrote:

## Source 15.16

*Today's women are little different from their medieval ancestors. They too might have two jobs – running a home and family as well as holding down a paid job in a factory, an office, in a shop, or in the professions. Men are rarely expected to do that.*

The EOC has tried to redress the situation by issuing posters like this.

## Source 15.17

## Activities

1 Have any important steps been taken to improve the position of women at work since 1945? **(KU)**

2 How effective have these steps been? Justify your answer. **(KU)**

3 How valuable is Maggy Meade-King's article (Source 15.14) for finding out about the problems faced by women at work in the 1980s? Give reasons for your answer. **(ENQ)**

4 Why, in your opinion, have women still not achieved equality with men at work? **(KU)**

5 Topic for class debate: 'Women will never achieve equality at work'.

**Section C 1945 to the present**

# Shipbuilding since 1945

The Second World War (1939–1945) brought an end to the troubles of the shipbuilding industry. The Clyde, in particular, gained from the need for warships. Shipyards in Dumbartonshire alone built two battleships, two aircraft carriers, three cruisers and 29 destroyers. Aberdeen yards built 114 ships, mainly landing craft, frigates and mine-sweepers.

Even when the war ended, the good times continued.

| **Source 15.18** | An extract from The Third Statistical Account for Dumbartonshire, 1959. |

*There has never been a shortage of orders. 1951 was a record year. At the end of 1955 firms were claiming that their berths were fully booked for four years. Tankers were most common (in some years 60%) and they seem likely to play a large part for many years to come.*

A warning was given, however, at this time.

| **Source 15.19** | A further account from The Third Statistical Account for Dumbartonshire, 1959. |

*Output might well have been higher. It has been related in recent years to the supply of steel, the supply of man-power and the rate of work. This in turn is affected by rules about which workers do which jobs. Uncertain delivery dates and rising costs may affect the order books.*

| **Source 15.20** | This table shows how Britain's share of shipping launched in the world has changed. |

| Year | % of ships launched |
| --- | --- |
| 1945 | 50 |
| 1957 | 20 |
| 1971 | 5 |
| 1985 | 2 |

As a result of the loss of orders to foreign yards, many shipyards closed.

Shipbuilding ended altogether in other areas, such as Dundee and Aberdeen. For workers in the industry, the result was unemployment. Only yards which adopted modern technology survived. The most important change was to weld ships together, instead of joining the steel plates with rivets. The best yards welded prefabricated sections, under cover; this made for faster and cheaper shipbuilding.

**Source** 15.21 This map compares the Clyde shipyards in 1914 and 1971.

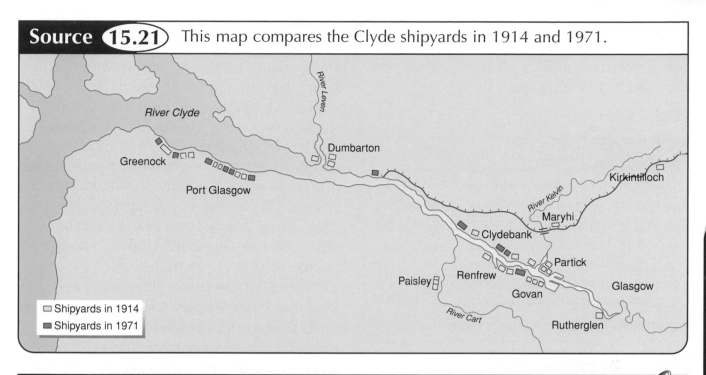

River Clyde

River Leven

Greenock

Dumbarton

Port Glasgow

Kirkintilloch

River Kelvin

Maryhi

Clydebank

Partick

Paisley

Renfrew

Glasgow

Govan

River Cart

Rutherglen

☐ Shipyards in 1914
■ Shipyards in 1971

F/G LEVEL

CREDIT LEVEL

## Activities

**1** What were the results of the Second World War for shipbuilding? **(KU)**

**2** What was the most important problem facing British shipbuilding after 1945? **(KU)**

# Shipbuilding problems after 1945

British yards shared in the great post-war boom that lasted till 1955. Sandy Stephen came into his family shipbuilding firm on the Clyde at this time.

**Source** 15.22 Quoted in Pagnamenta and Overy, 'All Our Working Days', 1984.

*Everything was very easy. People were able to make ends meet, we were able to make money. We could, within reason, ask what we liked for our ships. There were underlying problems, which while we were making money didn't really rear their ugly heads till later.*

A world slump hit shipbuilding after 1955, but while foreign yards recovered afterwards, British yards did not. World output trebled in the next ten years, but British output remained static. In 1963, the Conservative Government announced special grants and credit schemes, but still yards closed. In 1965 the large, modernised Fairfields yard went bankrupt. The new Labour Government did two things: it partly took over the yard with public money pumped in and new management attempted to tackle the old problems of productivity, demarcation and manning levels through granting secure employment and better pay; and it set up a Government inquiry to find out the real causes of the industry's problems.

The Geddes Report (1966) gave the problems faced by shipbuilding as:

CREDIT LEVEL

management's attitudes to markets, men and money had been short-term; individual firms were too small to deal effectively with customers and suppliers.

It also said:

## Source 15.23   The Geddes Report

*The past is very much alive in the minds of the workers in the industry and coupled with the general lack of confidence in the future of the industry it has bred a deep feeling of insecurity which is at the root of most of the demarcation disputes and practices in the industry which are commonly known as 'restrictive'.*

In one way, government help made it even more difficult to deal with 'restrictive' practices.

## Source 15.24   From the Commission on Industrial Relations, 1971.

*Financial assistance has had an adverse effect on industrial relations by encouraging the belief that public support [money] would be forthcoming whatever difficulties the companies got into.*

The Conservative Government's policy of refusing aid to 'lame ducks' was ended by a 'work in' at the Upper Clyde yards in 1971. This led to a nationalisation of the shipbuilding industry by the next Labour Government in 1977. Even then the industry's troubles were not over. In 1977, British Shipbuilders employed 86 000 but lost £106m; in 1982, under Mrs Thatcher, they employed only 66 000, but still lost £100m.

Among the innovations tried was the introduction of welding, at first using oxy-acetylene torches, and later electric arc welding. At first the steel hull plates were welded, replacing the trades of rivetting, and caulking (making the ship watertight by sealing any gaps with pitch). Lithgow's yard at Greenock even built very large ships in two parts on adjoining slipways and welded the complete bow and stern sections together to get round the problem of a small yard. Similarly, to save design costs, UCS pioneered standard design cargo ships to cut costs in the drawing office. Yarrows specialised in warships, and pioneered glass-fibre hulls as well as sophisticated electronic navigation and weapons systems; they were one of the first yards to cover in complete slipways on which the ships were built. But even Yarrows are still forced to lay off men from time to time.

Opinions have been divided over the causes of this decline.

## Source 15.25   Sir Leonard Redshaw, who managed Vickers' shipyards.

*There were plenty of good managers, have no doubt. But the atmosphere under which they had to work was demarcation and restrictive practices. I decided to pull my company out of building tankers, because they could build tankers on the continent with twenty per cent less man-hours than we could build them, purely because of British trade union practices.*

**Source 15.26**

Sandy Stephen, managing director of Alexander Stephen, the Govan shipbuilders, until 1966.

*I think one has to blame the management at that time for not taking more vigorous action. It's easy to blame the unions now, but the unions were not wholly to blame. With hindsight we should really have tackled all those demarcations vigorously, and they were capable of solution when things were good. But once things turned difficult, then it's very hard to get things right.*

**Source 15.27**

A Clydeside shop steward.

*If they had given better job security, sick pay, pensions, better working conditions, and that was possible with the vast profits they made, then in my opinion they could have won the co-operation of the workers. But they felt that gaffers wore bowler hats, and had the divine right to rule, and naturally if the management attitude is of that nature, then the workers react in a not very positive manner.*

**Source 15.28**

Graham Day, a Canadian, appointed Chairman of British Shipbuilders in 1983.

*British shipbuilding had not developed in plant terms, in work practice terms on the shop floor, in non-shipbuilding management skill terms, in marketing expertise, the way competitive industries in Sweden, Germany and certainly Japan had.*

## Activities

1 How did Government attitudes towards shipbuilding change between 1945 and the 1980s? **(KU)**

2 Did nationalisation solve shipbuilding's problems? Give reasons for your answer. **(KU)**

3 'Shipbuilding occupies a key position'. Explain changes in shipbuilding 1920–45. (Note for this answer you should write a short essay of several paragraphs). **(KU)**

4 Study Sources 15.25 to 15.28. Which of them gives the most valuable account of the causes of the decline of the British shipbuilding industry? Justify your answer. **(ENQ)**

5 Explain the main reasons for the decline of British shipbuilding. **(KU)**

**Group Activity**

Get into groups of about six. Each group represents a shipyard. Half of each group are its managers; the other half are its shop stewards, each representing a different one of its unions. Your task is to persuade Graham Day (the teacher)

a) why your yard should receive the £50m he has to invest, and

b) why yours should not be the yard he has to close!

(The teacher may wish to work this as a Balloon Night, with several rounds.)

# 16 Transport since 1945

FOUNDATION/GENERAL LEVEL

## The car is king

In the 50 years since the Second World War ended, motor cars have become more popular than ever. One reason for this is the continued improvement in technology.

Arthur Evans wrote in 1983:

**Source 16.1** — From **Arthur Evans**, 'The Motor Car', 1983.

*In the fifties and sixties the ideal was speed with style; in the seventies this was replaced by safety with economy. Research made cars more reliable. Improved designs increased speeds and improved fuel consumption.*

**Source 16.2** — The results of these changes are shown in these three British small cars.

◆ **The Morris Minor** *(1949).*
  *Rear wheel drive; 1000cc engine*
  *Cruising speed: 70mph*

◆ **The BMC Mini** *(1959).*
  *Front wheel drive; 850cc transverse engine*
  *Cruising speed: 70mph*

◆ **The Austin Mini Metro** *(1980).*
  *Front wheel drive; 1100cc transverse engine*
  *Cruising speed: 70mph*

*(Transverse engines saved space and gave better road-holding.)*

The Morris Minor.

The BMC Mini.

The Austin Mini Metro.

As cars and other road vehicles improved, they became more widely used.

**Source 16.3**

This table shows the increase in the number of road vehicles in Britain since 1945. Data comes from Government Figures from Official Handbooks.

| | 1945 | 1955 | 1971 | 1986 | 1997 |
|---|---|---|---|---|---|
| Cars (& vans) | 1.52 | 3.61 | 12.83 | 18.80 | 22.83 |
| Motorcycles | 0.70* | 0.90* | 1.00 | 1.10 | 0.63 |
| Buses & taxis | 0.04* | 0.05* | 0.07 | 0.10 | 0.79 |
| Lorries | 0.49 | 1.14 | 1.60 | 1.70 | 2.72 |
| Total | 3.11 | 6.15 | 15.50 | 21.70 | 26.97 |

(Figures in millions)
* Estimates

The growth of road traffic (5 per cent a year by 1986 – doubling every 14 years) has had several results. One is the increase in goods and people travelling by road. By 1986, 82 per cent of passenger journeys were by car/taxi; 9 per cent by bus; 8 per cent by rail and less than 1 per cent by air. The figures for goods were similar, with water transport taking the place of buses.

One result of more traffic was huge traffic jams. Another result is shown in Source 16.5.

**Source 16.4** A traffic jam.

**Source 16.5** A car accident.

## Activities

1 In what three ways did new technology improve cars built since 1945? **(KU)**

2 Study the table (Source 16.3). What type of road vehicle grew most quickly in popularity after 1945? Give figures /evidence to support your answer. **(KU)**

3 Why are the figures in the table reliable, overall? **(ENQ)**

4 Which parts of the table, if any, are not reliable? **(ENQ)**

**FOUNDATION/GENERAL LEVEL**

# Motor cars: problems of popularity

Problems following the growth of road traffic had long been known. By the 1960s they were becoming serious. In 1963 the Buchanan Report was published by the Government. See Source 16.6.

Its main recommendation was the separation of car and pedestrian traffic. One way this could be done would be the building of 'pedestrian precincts', where cars are banned and people can walk about freely. It also wanted the motorway network to be expanded considerably, and the flow of traffic in towns to be more controlled, for example, by one way streets.

**Source** **16.6** By 1971 the motorway network looked like this.

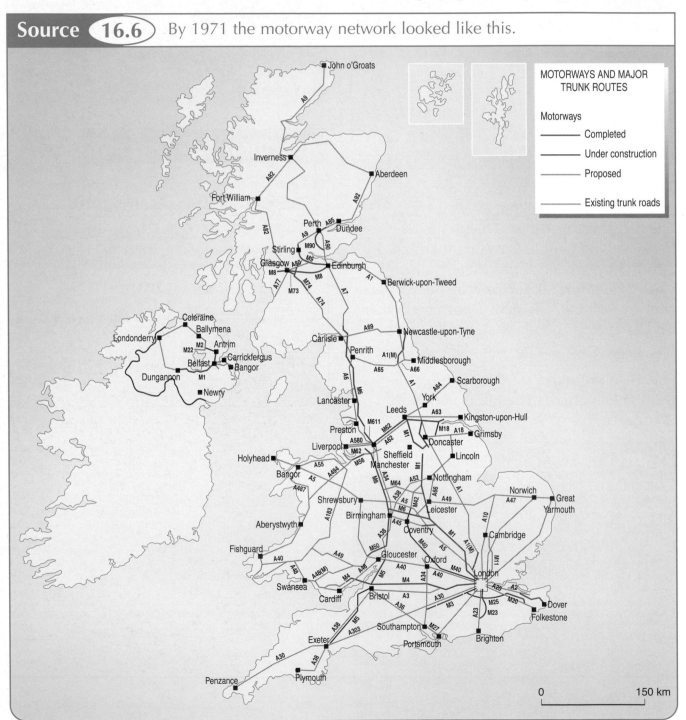

**Section C 1945 to the present**

**Source** 16.7 An extract from the Buchanan Report.

*At present there are in Great Britain about 16.4 million families and 6.6 million motor cars. There is no doubt that the desire to own a car is both widespread and intense. The most rapid increase will come sooner rather than later, for there are many families who are almost able to afford a car. By the year 2010 it is expected that the total number of cars will be over four times what it was in 1962.*

By this time, the Government was committed to developing road transport, and motorways in particular.

**Source** 16.8 From the 'Official Handbook', 1973.

*A large and steadily expanding road-building programme has been in progress since 1955. Public expenditure on new and improved roads in Great Britain is estimated at over £570m in 1972–3.*

*A government programme aims to complete by the early 1980s a network of 3 500 miles of trunk routes, including 2 000 miles of motorway, serving the main ports, airports and industrial centres and linking remote regions to the motorway network. In the interests of improving the environment, long-distance and in particular heavy goods traffic is being diverted from many towns and villages.*

This policy was continued in the 1980s.

**Source** 16.9 'Official Handbook', 1988.

*Following a review of the motorway and trunk road programme in England in 1987, 82 new schemes with a total cost of £689m were added to the programme, increasing it to some 370 schemes worth some £5 000m. Bypasses and relief roads account for about 50 per cent of these schemes.*

## Activities

1 What changes did the Buchanan Report warn about?

2 What solutions did it recommend?

3 How useful is Source 16.8 as evidence about road transport in the 1970s?

## Railways: the struggle for survival

The railways played an important role during the Second World War, but by 1945 they were in serious need of repair and improvement.

In 1947, the Government nationalised the railways, seeing that the Second World War had added to their problems of competing with increasing road traffic. British Railways, later British Rail, found that public ownership did not solve their difficulties. Indeed, the lack of investment made life even more difficult.

The post-war Labour Government tried to encourage co-operation between rail and road, to provide the most efficient transport service. The hope was that the nationalised railways would work with a nationalised road haulage service. This did not happen, because too much road transport was in lorries owned by private firms.

There was some investment in modernising railways in the 1950s, in the form of new, diesel locomotives, better tracks and signalling. But two further factors contributed to the continued decline of the railways. The first was the denationalisation of road haulage in 1953 and the second was the closures of lines and stations made during the 1960s following the report by Dr Beeching.

Railways tried to become more efficient but faced big problems (Source 16.10).

**Source 16.10**   Richard Tames summed up the railways' situation.

*The railways' efforts to introduce modern methods often created unemployment, leading to labour troubles and strikes, which in turn slowed modernisation. The closing of stations and unprofitable lines angered the public. Old debts, giving higher wages and financing modernisation has meant that the railways consistently run at a loss. Railways still have a role to play – the problem is to find it and make it a profitable one.*

### Activities

1   Describe the state of the railways at the end of the Second World War. **(KU)**

2   Did the post-war Labour Government take any important steps to help railways? **(KU)**

3   Why did the railways decline in the 1950s and 1960s? **(KU)**

# 17

# Home and health

## Housing

In 1945 Britain was 1 250 000 houses short and the Government planned to build 300 000 a year. By 1950, less than a million had been built and £150 million was spent on prefabricated houses (prefabs) of corrugated iron and asbestos. They were only intended to last five years.

**Source 17.1** Prefabs in 1961.

Most of the houses built in Scotland in the 1950s were council houses but the 1960s and early 1970s saw a boom in private house building. As city slums were pulled down, many people were moved to New Towns like East Kilbride where tower

**Source 17.2** In this account, a woman describes her experience as a young girl in Airdrie.

*Our single storey building was in the shape of a hollow rectangle with a gap at one corner. Around 40 families shared the drying greens and outside toilets. Our single-end was in the far corner. My parents' bed was in one of the recesses and my bed and my baby brother's cot was in the other. A wardrobe and sideboard took up the far wall. An armchair stood on each side of the fire and an oil-cloth covered the table and four chairs made the rest of the furniture. The iron sink was under the window and the gas cooker beside it. A gas light above the fire gave us light. We did not have enough points to put us at the top of the council housing list, but there was a gas leak which nearly killed us and we got emergency rehousing in a prefab.*

*Our prefab had white walls and a front and side door. The electric light was such a novelty John and I had to be lifted up to switch it off and on. The kitchen had two sinks and the wringer could sit between them. The living room was as large as the single-end and beyond it was a lobby with the front door, two bedrooms and bathroom off it. Having an inside toilet and a real bath was a treat. We had our own front and back garden and a walk-in coal shed made of corrugated iron. We would have trouble with dampness and condensation in the ten years we lived there, but in 1952 when we moved in, it seemed like a palace.*

93

blocks became more common. Despite more than five million houses being built since 1945, one million homes still had no inside lavatory and 800 000 had no bath in 1976.

| Source **17.3** | The 15-storey Frazer River Tower in East Kilbride. |

## Activities

**1** Use Source 17.2.

Draw a table comparing as many aspects of the Airdrie girl's two houses as you can.

|  | Single-End | Prefab |
|---|---|---|
| rooms | 1 | |
| light | | electric |
| toilet | | |

**2** Why did the girl think the prefab was 'like a palace'? **(KU)**

**3** She wrote this account almost 35 years later. Do you think this makes good evidence? Explain your answer. **(ENQ)**

**4** What types of houses can you see in Source 17.3? **(KU)**

## New towns

By 1971 there were 32 New Towns with a total population of 900 000. They cost £759 million but were well planned, each with a Development Corporation to look after and plan the town, ensuring that all the necessary amenities were there for the people. As well as having a town centre, each neighbourhood had shops, schools and a community hall. There was safety for pedestrians and plenty of space for children. The prosperity of the towns was ensured by ample encouragement for new industries. Source 17.3 shows East Kilbride, the oldest of Scotland's New Towns.

## Home ownership

One of the biggest changes since 1945 has been in the number of people buying their own homes. This trend was increased in the early 1980s when the Conservative Government introduced legislation to allow council tenants to buy their homes. This policy has not pleased the many councils who have lost their best housing stock and do not have money to replace it.

## Source 17.4 Changes in the housing market.

| | Scotland | England | South-east |
|---|---|---|---|
| **Tenure (% 1988)** | | | |
| Owner-occupied | 45 | 67 | 68 |
| Rented – local authority/new town | 46 | 23 | 21 |
| Private rental or tied | 6 | 8 | 8 |
| Rented – housing association | 3 | 3 | 3 |
| **New Dwellings (% change 1981–88)** | | | |
| Private enterprise | +28 | +63 | +67 |
| Housing associations | –34 | –45 | –60 |
| Local authorities etc. | –60 | –71 | –67 |
| **Market Value (% increase 1981–87)** | | | |
| All housing stock | 102 | 140 | 181 |

However, not all tenants wish to buy their houses. Many people are still living in unsatisfactory conditions. Source 17.5 explains one of the main problems.

## Source 17.5

An extract from Glasgow District Council 'Housing Conditions Survey', 1989.

*Nearly half the District Council housing stock was built between 1945 and 1964. This was an era of low fuel costs ... when it was assumed the tenants would be able to heat their houses cheaply. The combination of unemployment, rising fuel prices and poorly ventilated houses with inefficient and expensive heating systems has led to high levels of condensation in many groups of council houses. For instance 35 per cent of Glasgow District Council early post-war tenements have condensation.*

## Activities

1  In what ways was a prefab better than a single-end? **(KU)**

2  Why was a prefab not completely satisfactory? **(KU)**

3  Look at the sources about East Kilbride. Now write an advertisement to encourage families to move there. **(KU)**

4  What changes have taken place in housing ownership in Scotland in the 1980s? **(KU)**

5  How fully do sources 17.1, 17.2, 17.3 and 17.5, show changes in housing in Scotland since 1945. **(ENQ)**

**Group Activity**
**Either**
Prepare a questionnaire of at least 10 questions to investigate housing in your area
**or**
Prepare a case for and against the sale of council houses to private ownership.

# Health

Although 22 million workers were covered by the National Insurance scheme between the wars, their wives and children were not. With a charge of 3s 6d (17.5p) for a home visit and extra for medicines, it is not surprising that the poor rarely saw a doctor. Dentists were only seen when a tooth needed to be extracted. Of the six million people who needed spectacles, many had to make do with a 6d (2.5p) pair bought in Woolworths.

Following on from the Beveridge Report, the 1946 National Health Act planned:

◆ A completely free medical service for all – doctors, prescriptions, dentists, hospitals, etc.

◆ All hospitals were nationalised

◆ 20 Regional Hospital Boards organised and ran hospitals

◆ Local authorities were responsible for ambulances, maternity and child welfare, home nursing and school medicals

◆ 138 separate Executive Councils dealt with doctors' pensions, chemists etc.

**Source** 17.7

This account from J. Cootes, 'The Making of the Welfare State', 1966, tells what happened when the National Health Service started in July 1948.

*Surgeries were invaded like bargain basements. The 'family doctor' service was, at last, for everyone and they rushed to make use of it. Dentists were soon booked solid for many months ahead, and there was even a five months' wait for spectacles. Before long Bevan (the Health Minister) had to make a special appeal to the public to use the National Health Service sensibly. By the end of the first year 187 million prescriptions, 8 500 000 dental treatments and 5 500 000 pairs of glasses had been issued.*

Ninety-five per cent of the population used the new service, with only 6 000 out of 240 000 hospital beds being kept for those

**Source** 17.6

'Dentist says if there are any more of you thinking of fitting one another up with National Health teeth for Christmas presents you've had it.'

**Source 17.8** A specialist operating ward in a present-day hospital.

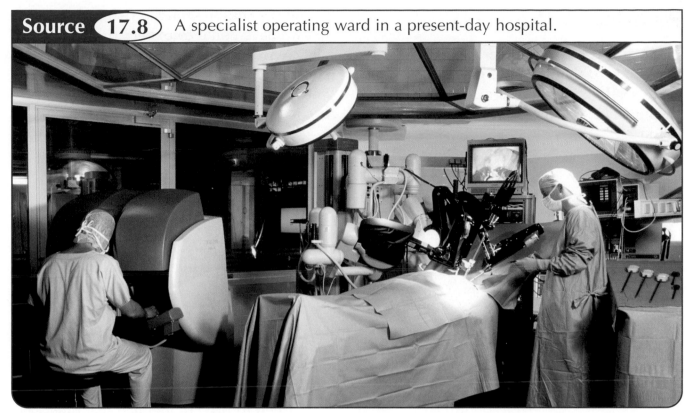

who wanted to pay so they did not have to wait for treatment.

This service was the envy of the world but it was very expensive and by 1951 those who could afford it had to pay for prescription charges, part of their dental treatment and spectacles.

The National Health Service has had important successes. Killer diseases such as tuberculosis (TB) have almost been wiped out and people live longer.

In 1931 male life expectancy was 58 and female was 62. By 1970 this had risen to 68 for men and almost 75 for women.

**Source 17.9**

| Life expectancy (years) | | |
| --- | --- | --- |
| | 1931 | 1970 |
| Men | 58.4 | 68.6 |
| Women | 62.5 | 74.9 |

Different killer diseases such as cancer and heart disease have increased, but these may be partly our own fault as prosperity has led to an increase in smoking and unhealthy eating.

## Activities

1 Which two groups of people were not covered by the National Insurance scheme before the war? **(KU)**

2 How did the National Health Act 1946 change this? **(KU)**

3 In what ways does Source 17.7 show you that the NHS (National Health Service) was needed? **(KU)**

4 Is Source 17.6 useful evidence about the National Health Service? Explain your answer. **(ENQ)**

**Interview/Group Work**
Make up a questionnaire of at least eight questions to ask an old person what difference the NHS made to them.

# Results of the NHS

There is no doubt that the NHS made a difference to the health of children. For the years 1959–60 and 1960–61, Sighthill Health Centre, Edinburgh provided the following.

**Source 17.10** — Sighthill Health Centre, Annual Report 1960–1.

| Vaccination and immunisation | | |
| --- | --- | --- |
| | 1959–60 | 1960–61 |
| Smallpox | 103 | 101 |
| Whooping cough | 262 | 292 |
| Diphtheria | 156 | 193 |
| Polio | 491 | 305 |

| Free or cheap welfare foods supplied each week | | |
| --- | --- | --- |
| | 1959–60 | 1960–61 |
| Tins of National Dried Milk | 70 | 55 |
| Bottles of cod liver oil | 18 | 21 |
| Packets of vitamins A & D | 10 | 14 |
| Bottles of concentrated orange juice | 124 | 131 |

Funding the NHS has always been a problem as only about 20 per cent of the money comes from insurance payments and the rest from general taxation. These government figures show the increase.

**Source 17.11**

| Year | Cost (in millions of pounds) |
| --- | --- |
| 1949 | 388 |
| 1958 | 700 |
| 1967 | 1 400 |
| 1971 | 2 270 |
| 1976 | 5 470 |
| 1981 | 11 944 |
| 1985 | 16 304 |

One of the reasons for the rising cost is that we have come to expect the best medical treatment, but the advances in medicine have also contributed, as a Wolverhampton surgeon reported in *The Sunday Times*, 14 February 1982.

**Source 17.12**

*We can now save a limb crushed in a traffic accident but it may take four or more operations, five months in hospital and cost £20 000. A few years ago we would have cut the leg off and it would have cost £100.*

It is, therefore, no wonder that people are constantly talking about a crisis in the NHS with increasing waiting lists for hospital beds. By 1985, some four million people had turned to private medical insurance as a way of avoiding these.

**Source 17.13** — Waiting room in a modern hospital.

## Activities

1 Write a paragraph explaining who needed a National Health Service and why. **(KU)**

2 What services did the NHS bring? **(KU)**

3 In what ways has the NHS helped keep babies and children healthy? **(KU)**

4 a) Make a list of the successes and problems of the NHS.

b) How successful do you think it is? Give reasons. **(KU)**

5 Compare Sources 17.12 and 17.13 as evidence of problems of the NHS. **(ENQ)**

CREDIT LEVEL

# 18 New politics – new parties

## The vote for all

The efforts of the ordinary people in the First World War earned the vote for all men aged 21 and over and women over 30. In 1928 this was extended to all adults. The voting age was not reduced to 18 until 1969.

## Choosing an MP

When some working men first gained the vote at the end of the nineteenth century, they had to decide whether to vote for the Liberals or Conservatives. The rich landowners had most influence in the Conservative Party while industrialists and the middle class had most influence on the Liberals. Most working-class voters supported the Liberals but they were unhappy because the Liberals seemed to help the employers more often than the workers.

What the workers needed was a party of their own. In the 1880s William Morris and H. M. Hyndman sold over 100 000 copies of a book called *Socialism for All*. Its ideas have been summed up in this way.

**Source 18.1** An extract from Hyman Shapiro, 'Keir Hardie and the Rise of the Labour Party', 1972.

*It pointed out that every year £300 million were paid as wages, but £1 000 million went to the capitalists (bosses) as rent, profit and interest. It called for the Government to take over railways and land as a first step to taking over all industries and banks to nationalise them. The immediate task, though, was to build good houses for the workers, reduce their working day to eight hours, give work to the unemployed, and provide free education for all, with one free meal in school every day.*

Many trade unionists agreed with these ideas and in 1888 a Scottish miner, Keir Hardie, formed a Scottish Labour Party in Glasgow. He stood as a candidate for Parliament in Mid-Lanark that year and made his view of working-class Liberal MPs clear in this speech.

**Source 18.2** Keir Hardie, 1888.

*The man who poses as a Liberal, and yet refuses to support shorter working hours, an improvement in the homes of the people, ... relief work for the unemployed and the return of land to its rightful owners, may call himself what he pleases, but he is an enemy and must be opposed.*

He did not win in 1888 but became MP for West Ham in London in 1892. The next year English and Scottish groups joined together to become the Independent Labour Party. In 1900 they joined with some trade union groups to become the Labour Representation Committee. A Scot from Lossiemouth, James Ramsay MacDonald, was made secretary. They aimed to put working men into the House of Commons and in the 1906 election the LRC won 29 seats.

The Liberals were quick to realise that these MPs, who now called themselves the Labour Party, would take votes from them. In the years before 1914 the Liberal government passed many reforms.

## The Labour Party Since 1918

Support for the Labour Party continued to grow after the First World War as the table below shows. The number of active members increased as did the number of voters. The Liberals lost support.

**Source 18.4**

| Year | Party Members | Votes | Seats | Events |
|------|---------------|-------|-------|--------|
| 1910 | 140 000 | 500 000 | 42 | |
| 1918 | 220 000 | 2 350 000 | 57 | |
| 1924 | 350 000 | 5 000 000 | 191 | 1st Labour Govt |
| 1929 | 200 000 | 8 000 000 | 288 | 2nd Labour Govt |
| 1945 | 300 000 | 11 500 000 | 394 | Labour Govt (maj) |

In 1924 the First Labour Government, under Ramsay MacDonald, did not have a majority and only lasted ten months. The disaster of the 1926 General Strike cut trade union membership from 8 to 5 million, and showed that only Parliament could improve conditions for the working class. (You will find more about the General Strike in Chapter 19.) The 1927 Trade Disputes Act said that trade unions could only give a part of members' subscriptions to the Labour Party if members asked in writing. This cut the Labour Party's income by 25 per cent.

In 1929 the Second Labour Government still had no majority and could not deal with the economic problems facing them. They resigned in 1931, though MacDonald stayed on as Prime Minister in a National Government with the Conservatives.

**Source 18.3**

This cartoon of 1908 gives the Labour Party view of the Liberals' social reforms.

CAUSE AND EFFECT.

SOCIAL LEGISLATION 1906-1908
TRADE DISPUTES ACT
WORKMEN'S COMPENSATION ACT
SCHOOL-CHILDREN'S MEALS ACT
OLD AGE PENSIONS
UNEMPLOYED GRANT £300 000
MINERS EIGHT HOURS BILL

*Keir Hardie: 'Look at that list, Mr. Bull—not one of them would have been passed if it hadn't been for our Labour Party!' (a cartoon of 1908).*

It was 1945 before the Third Labour Government came to power with a majority which let them pass the Beveridge Reforms which set up the Welfare State. Since then, Labour and Conservative have been the two main parties of government.

**F/G LEVEL**

**CREDIT LEVEL**

## Activities

**1**   Which party did most workers vote for at the end of the nineteenth century? **(KU)**

**2**   What were a) the immediate tasks and b) the long-term aims of socialists? **(KU)**

**3**   Why would Keir Hardie and workers support these ideas? **(KU)**

**4**   Why is Source 18.2 valuable evidence about the early Labour Party? **(ENQ)**

**5**   What is the evidence that the Labour Party became stronger after 1918? Use Source 18.4.

# Political Parties since 1945

The coming of adult suffrage led to political parties issuing a manifesto – a statement of the policies they support.

**Source** **18.5** Party Policies

| Area | Labour | Conservative |
|---|---|---|
| Economy | Plan development. Nationalise industries, profits to nation | Cut government spending. Let private industry get on and create wealth |
| Taxes | Take from rich to help less well-off | Keep taxes low, let people spend own money |
| Social Services | Free health and social services, low prescription charges | Encourage private medicine Encourage people to work |
| Education | Want comprehensive schools. End fee-paying schools | Keep selective and fee-paying schools |
| Trade Unions | Work with and strengthen unions | Reduce trade union powers |

At general elections, party members in each constituency help their candidate by going round the doors and spreading publicity.

Many people in the country do not support either of the major parties. In the 1980s the Liberal Party joined with the SDP (Social Democratic Party) – which had been formed in 1981 by right-wing Labour MPs to gain votes from those who thought that the Labour Party was going too far towards socialism and that the Conservatives were too right-wing.

In Scotland and Wales, Nationalist Parties have appeared because they want to keep their own way of life and think British governments do not do enough for their areas. The SNP was formed in 1934 and won its first parliamentary seat in a by-election in Motherwell in 1945. In 1949 two million Scots signed a petition asking for Home Rule. The fortunes of the SNP declined during the prosperity of the 1950s and early 1960s but as unemployment increased so did its support, with Winnie Ewing winning a by-election in Hamilton in 1967.

**Source 18.6** The seats won by each party in election in Scotland since 1970.

| Year | Labour | Conservative | Liberal | SNP |
|------|--------|--------------|---------|-----|
| 1970 | 44 | 23 | 3 | 1 |
| 1974 (Feb) | 40 | 21 | 3 | 7 |
| 1974 (Oct) | 41 | 16 | 3 | 11 |
| 1979 | 44 | 22 | 3 | 2 |
| 1983 | 41 | 21 | 8 | 2 |
| 1987 | 50 | 10 | 9 | 3 |
| 1992 | 49 | 11 | 9 | 3 |
| 1997 | 56 | 0 | 10 | 6 |
| 2001 | 55 | 1 | 10 | 5 |

The discovery of oil off Scotland's coast gave the SNP grounds for saying that Scotland could finance its own government from oil revenues. By the early 1970s, the SNP was demanding independence. In 1973 a Royal Commission suggested a Scottish Assembly with limited control over housing, transport (not British Rail), law, local government and education. In 1974 official government figures revealed the value of the oil from taxation was £3 billion a year. The SNP cry 'Scotland's oil' was one many voters seemed to agree with.

In 1979 a referendum was held on the Assembly proposals. Only 62.9 per cent of people voted with 1 230 937 (51.6 per cent) in favour and 1 153 502 (48.4 per cent) against. However, the Government had said beforehand that 40 per cent of all voters would need to approve of the changes and only 32.85 per cent had, so devolution was dropped for the time being.

**Source 18.7** The percentage of votes for the SNP in recent elections and the number of seats they gained.

| Year | Number of votes | % of votes | Seats won |
|------|-----------------|------------|-----------|
| 1970 | 306 802 | 11.4 | 1 |
| 1974 (Feb) | 633 180 | 21.9 | 7 |
| 1974 (Oct) | 839 617 | 30.4 | 11 |
| 1979 | 504 259 | 18.4 | 2 |
| 1983 | 332 045 | 11.8 | 2 |
| 1987 | 416 473 | 14 | 3 |
| 1992 | 629 564 | 21.5 | 3 |
| 1997 | 621 550 | 22.1 | 6 |
| 2001 | 464 305 | 20.1 | 5 |

In the 1983 election the SNP argued as follows.

**Source 18.8** A quote from the Scottish Nationalist Party, 1983.

*Whichever English party wins the election, regional aid will be redirected to the Midlands of England, to Scotland's disadvantage ... Never has the need for an independent Scottish Parliament and a Scottish government been greater.*

*Only with our own Government will Scotland have the will and the resources to reverse our economic decline and end mass unemployment ... to remove all nuclear weapons from our soil, ... to tackle the appalling social conditions in which many of our people have to live.*

Since 1983 the Labour manifesto had promised an Assembly with tax raising powers. When SNP candidate Jim Sillars won the Govan by-election in November 1988, its fortune seemed to be improving at the expense of the Labour Party.

Trade unions, churches, prominent people and all parties, except the Conservatives, agreed to set up a Constitutional Convention to look at devolution. The SNP withdrew in February 1989 because it was offered only 8 per cent of the seats, which meant that Labour would dominate the Convention. To many people it looked as if the SNP was being obstructive but it believed that, as usual, it was being unfairly treated by the two major parties. The system of 'first past the post' voting in British elections helps the major parties, as shown by the 2001 General Election results.

CREDIT LEVEL

**Source 18.9**

Sir Sean Connery joins SNP party leader John Swinney in the run-up to the 2001 General Election.

**Source 18.10** — 2001 General Election results

| Party | Votes ('000) | No. of MPs | Average vote per MP |
|---|---|---|---|
| Labour | 10 725 | 412 | 26 031 |
| Conservative | 8 358 | 166 | 50 349 |
| Liberal Democrats | 4 813 | 52 | 92 557 |
| SNP | 464 | 5 | 92 800 |
| UK Independence | 391 | 0 | |
| Ulster Unionist | 217 | 6 | 36 166 |
| Plaid Cymru | 196 | 4 | 49 000 |

As Britain moved into the late 1990s the role of the SNP and other nationalist parties remained an important issue, particularly in the light of the setting up of separate assemblies in Scotland and Wales.

# A parliament for Scotland

In September 1997 the people of Scotland were again asked in a referendum to show how they felt about a separate parliament for Scotland. A clear majority voted in favour of Scotland having her own parliament again, and elections were held in May 1999. The new Scottish Parliament met for the first time on 1st July 1999.

There were 129 members and the numbers in each party for the first parliament, and the second (elected May 2003) are shown in Source 18.11.

**Source 18.11** — Distribution of seats in the Scottish Parliament

| Party | 1999 | 2003 |
|---|---|---|
| Labour | 56 | 50 |
| SNP | 35 | 27 |
| Conservative & Union | 18 | 18 |
| Liberal Democrats | 17 | 17 |
| Independent | 1 | 3 |
| Scottish Socialists | 1 | 6 |
| Scottish Greens | 1 | 7 |
| Scottish Senior Citizens | | 1 |

## Activities

Rise of the Labour Party

1  Explain fully why a new 'Labour' party was formed at the end of the nineteenth century. **(KU)**

2  What effect did it have on other political parties? **(KU)**

Political parties since 1945

3  Why has there been support for the Scottish Nationalist Party since 1945? **(KU)**

4  Is Source 18.9 useful evidence about the Scottish National Party? **(ENQ)**

5  To what extent has the setting up of a separate Scottish pariament helped the (cause of) Scottish Nationalist Party? **(KU)**

**Group Activity**

Hold a mock-election with candidates from the different parties putting forward their case.

# 19 Trade unions since the 1850s

Trade unions are organisations of workers. Their aims are to obtain the best wages and best working conditions for their members. They do this by helping workers act together to convince employers to raise wages or to make the workplace safer. If the employers are unwilling to make changes, the workers may go on strike. This means they stop work so the employers cannot provide goods or services to sell at a profit.

## Craft unions 1850s–80s

From the 1850s to 1880s the only successful unions belonged to skilled workers or craftsmen. They were paid higher wages because of their skills and if they went on strike, employers did not find it easy to replace them with equally skilled men. Most people thought unskilled workers had no chance of winning a strike because there were always unemployed people who would be 'blacklegs' and take over their jobs.

In 1868 union representatives from the north and midlands of England met in Manchester and set up the Trades Union Conference (TUC). 40 delegates attended the TUC annual conference in 1869 representing over 250 000 workers.

## New unionism

This attitude changed because of two strikes at the end of the 1880s. In June 1888, match girls at Bryant and May's

match factories went on strike. They earned about 4 shillings (20p) a week, but the company often took back some of their wages as fines for such things as dropping matches or going to the toilet without permission. The matches were made with yellow phosphorous which gave many of the girls a cancer of the face which they called 'phossy' jaw. This caused the girls' faces to swell and their teeth to fall out, and it was often fatal. The use of this phosphorous was banned in other countries like America and Sweden. Source 19.1 shows match girls during their strike.

**Source** 19.1 The 1888 match girls' strike.

Campaigners such as Annie Besant, Catherine Booth and even George Bernard Shaw supported the match girls and encouraged the public to boycott (not to buy) matches made by Bryant and May. Their strike and the campaign in support of it were so successful that the company soon gave in and granted the match girls what they wanted.

In 1889 the London dockers went on strike. They only earned 5d (2p) per hour and were hired to load and unload ships, so were often lucky to get two days' work per week. They demanded 6d an hour 'the dockers' tanner', 8d (3p) for overtime and a minimum of four hours' work. They held processions and marches which won public sympathy.

The public were impressed by their good organisation and peaceful methods and a fund of nearly £100 000 was gathered (£30 000 from Australian dockers). They too won their strike.

These strikes led to 'new' unions of unskilled workers being formed. Bricklayers' labourers, textile workers and builders' labourers all formed unions in 1889 and 1890. Source 19.2 shows how the number of workers in trade unions changed between 1888 and 1978.

| Source 19.2 | British Trade Union Membership. |
|---|---|

| Year | Membership |
|---|---|
| 1888 | 750 000 |
| 1893 | 1 559 000 |
| 1900 | 2 002 000 |
| 1914 | 4 145 000 |
| 1920 | 8 347 000 |
| 1926 | 5 219 000 |
| 1928 | 4 806 000 |
| 1933 | 4 392 000 |
| 1938 | 6 003 000 |
| 1948 | 9 632 000 |
| 1958 | 9 639 000 |
| 1968 | 10 049 000 |
| 1978 | 12 173 000 |
| 1988 | 9 000 000 |
| 1998 | 7 100 000 |

Trade unions seemed to gain some improvement after 1906 when the Labour Party MPs helped pass laws to protect Trade Union funds.

From 1910 until 1914 trade was good and there was a series of strikes as workers tried to get their share of prosperity. Not all were successful but it looked as though things might change. In 1914 the Miners' Federation, National Federation of Transport Workers and National Union of Railwaymen formed a 'triple alliance' promising to help each other. The threat of a general strike was put aside with the start of the First World War in 1914.

In 1921, the miners called on their allies when the coalowners cut their wages. However, on 'Black' Friday, 15 April, the railwaymen and transport workers backed down. After a three month strike the miners had to accept lower wages. In 1925, employers wanted further wage cuts and this time the railwaymen and transport workers agreed not to move any coal when the miners went on strike. On 'Red' Friday, 31 July, the Government promised a £24 million subsidy for 9 months while the Samuel Commission looked at the coal industry. The Government also set up the Organisation for the Maintenance of Supplies (OMS) obtaining 100 000 volunteers to move essential goods if the strike took place.

# 1926 The general strike

The Royal Commission on mining recommended reorganisation, and an improvement in conditions but also said wage cuts were necessary. A. J. Cooke, the miners' leader, said 'Not a penny off the pay, not a minute on the day'. On 1 May 1926 the miners went on strike and the

Trades Union Congress called out workers from the Triple Alliance to support them. At midnight on 3 May the General Strike began with all transport, printing, dock, iron and steel workers being called out – around three million.

The OMS managed to keep essential supplies going as the photographs in Source 19.3 show.

Most newspapers stopped publishing although the Government and unions each published their own newspaper. For many people, BBC radio was their main source of news.

When the Government offered discussions on 12 May, the Trades Union Congress (TUC) called off the strike as they did not have the money for a long strike. The miners felt betrayed and stayed out for seven months before hunger drove them back to work.

| Source 19.3 | Volunteers carried out essential services during the General Strike. |
|---|---|

The following two sources describe how the General Strike affected workers and their families in Scotland.

| Source 19.4 | An extract from 'Weavers, Miners and the Open Book' by James Hutchison, 1986. |
|---|---|

*In Kilsyth the lock-outs lasted for seven months and caused severe hardship. There were about 400 applications for parish relief each week, about one-quarter of the town's ratepayers. This amounted to 10 shillings (50p) for the miner's wife and 3 shillings 6d (17.5p) for each child or about one half of the miner's existing poor wage. 950 school children were given two free meals per day for six days each week, usually broth for four of the days and mince and potatoes for the other two. The Kilsyth Co-operative society had 3500 members, about three-quarters of whom came from mining families. Co-op sales fell by 25 per cent during the lock-out.*

This account is by George Chalmers, the son of an Airdrie miner.

**Source 19.5**

*I was almost four that summer of the General Strike but I remember going with my father to the bing so we could pick bits of coal to put on the fire. It was a good job the summer was good so I could run about in my bare feet with the other children. I can remember queuing with my father each day at the Salvation Army soup kitchen for a bowl of soup and a piece of bread.*

FOUNDATION/GENERAL LEVEL

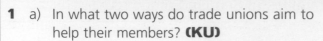

## Activities

**1** a) In what two ways do trade unions aim to help their members? **(KU)**

   b) What method can they use to force employers to listen to them? **(KU)**

**2** a) What type of union was successful in the 1870s?

   b) For what two reasons were they successful? **(KU)**

**3** a) Which two unions had successful strikes in 1888 and 1889?

   b) Why is it surprising they won?

   c) Explain why they were successful.

   e) What effect did this have on trade union membership (Source 19.2)? Explain why this would happen. **(KU)**

**4** a) Why did miners go on strike in 1926?

   b) Why did it become known as the 'General Strike'? **(KU)**

**5** How useful are the photographs in Source 19.3 as evidence about the General Strike? **(ENQ)**

# Contrasting views of the general strike

These sources give two different views of the General Strike.

**Source 19.6**

This is an article from 'The British Worker', which was published by the Trades Union Congress.

### WONDERFUL RESPONSE TO THE CALL
#### General Council's Message: Stand Firm and Keep Order

The workers' response has exceeded all expectations. The first day of the great General Strike is over. They have manifested their determination and unity to the whole world. They have resolved that the attempt of the mineowners to starve three million men, women and children into submission shall not succeed.

All the essential industries and all the transport services have been brought to a standstill. The only exception is that the distribution of milk and food has been permitted to continue. The Trades Union General Council is not making war on the people. It is anxious that the ordinary members of the public shall not be penalised for the unpatriotic conduct of the mineowners and the Government.

Never have the workers reponded with the greater enthusiasm to the end of their leaders.. The only difficulty that the General Council is experiencing, in fact, is in persuading those workers in the second line of defence to continue work until the withdrawal of their labour may be needed.

The Conservative Party was equally outspoken in its views on the strike.

**Source 19.7**

This extract is from a handbill published by the Conservative Party.

### THE GREAT "HOLD-UP"
**T.U.C. Threat to the Nation**
### STORY OF THE STRIKE
**What is the General Strike about?**

*The Commission reported that 7 out of every 10 tons of coal are being produced at a loss. It also saw a revision of wages was needed to save the industry.*

*The Government accepted the Report. The Coal Owners accepted it. The miners refused to work a second longer or take a penny less even as a temporary measure to prevent ruin.*

*The Government strove night and day to secure an agreement. While negotiations were going on the Trade Union Council (without consulting the workers) issued notices for a General Strike which would paralyse transport, factories, public services, printing works, and the entire business of the Country.*

*The Government then put in force its plans for maintaining food and milk supplies. It called upon all loyal people to offer help.*

*As Mr Baldwin said, "the Government found itself challenged with an alternative Government." This alternative Government is a small group of Trade Union leaders. It represents only a small section of the people.*

**THE GOVERNMENT STANDS FOR THE PEOPLE – THE PEOPLE WILL STAND BY THE GOVERNMENT**

# After the general strike

The miners had been the most militant and best organised trade union. Their defeat after such a long strike meant a decline in mining until the Second World War. The number of workers in trade unions dropped in the late 1920s and stayed low during the depression in the 1930s.

During those years, workers turned more to the Labour Party and in the 1931 General Election, 79 out of 154 Labour MPs were trade union MPs. Thirty-four of these were miners' MPs.

# After the Second World War

After the Second World War it soon became clear to many people that British industry was having trouble competing with other countries. Firms were using old fashioned machines which needed more workers and therefore cost more to run. Unions preferred to have this 'overmanning' as their members did not lose their jobs.

There were also problems with demarcation disputes where unions insisted certain jobs could only be done by their members. This might mean that in the shipyards, eight men from four trades did what three men could do more quickly and cheaply.

Craft unions also tried to protect their members' jobs by restricting the number of apprentices entering their trade. This would mean there would be enough work for existing members.

These practices often led to disputes in the workplace between the unions and employers.

From 1940 to 1951 it was compulsory for employers and trade unions to go before an arbitration tribunal if they could not settle disputes. After that time it could still be used if both sides agreed. Often the unions preferred to go on strike. If the strike was called by the union, it was called an official strike. The strikers were then entitled to weekly payments from the union's strike fund and could claim supplementary benefits from the Government for their families.

By the late 1950s many firms were trying to get round these problems by offering productivity agreements – better wages, benefits, etc. – if the unions would end restrictive practices like overmanning. In 1959 the Esso refinery at Fawley made such a productivity agreement with its workers and companies like ICI and the Steel Company of Wales soon followed them.

By the 1960s many workers felt that the national leadership of unions was out of touch with the needs of members. 95 per cent of all strikes were unofficial (did not have the backing of the union).

**Source 19.8** Average annual figures for official and unofficial strikes between 1964 and 1967.

| Type of Stoppage | Number of Stoppages | Number of Workers Involved | Number of Working Days Lost |
|---|---|---|---|
| Official strikes | 82 | 84 700 | 643 000 |
| Partly official (some unions recognised strike officially) | 2 | 600 | 6000 |
| Unofficial | 2125 | 663 300 | 1 857 000 |
| Others, e.g., lock-outs | 24 | 3200 | 24 000 |

These strikes affected not only the factory where the men went on strike but workers elsewhere. If workers in a factory making a component for a car went on strike it affected all the other workers making that kind of car.

In 1967 a Royal Commission on Industrial Relations was set up, but pressure from the unions prevented the Labour Government changing the law. In 1971 the Conservative Government passed the Industrial Relations Act which tried to make the collective agreements of employer and trade union binding by law. It also tried to supervise trade union rules and put an end to the 'closed shop' where workers doing certain jobs had to belong to a particular union. It also imposed a 60 day 'cooling off' period and insisted on a ballot of members before a strike could take place.

This led to a bitter miners' strike in 1972 – the first coalminers' strike since 1926. When the Conservative Government of Sir Edward Heath tried to bring in a policy to control incomes and limit wage increases this led to strikes by gas workers and civil servants in 1973. In November the miners banned overtime and from the beginning of 1974 there were power cuts in both houses and industry, with most workers on a three day week. When the miners went on an all out strike Heath called a general election, which he lost.

A new Labour Government was elected under Harold Wilson, which repealed the 1971 Industrial Relations Act and introduced a voluntary agreement between the Labour Government and the TUC, called the 'Social Contract'. This promised food subsidies and price controls.

Wages rose by 30 per cent during 1974–5, with prices not far behind. This inflation increased the prices of British goods and made it more difficult to sell British goods abroad. The Chancellor of the Exchequer, Denis Healey, was forced to restrict wage rises in 1975. His attempts to impose guidelines in the years following finally met

**Source 19.9** Harold Wilson addresses the 1974 TUC conference which established the 'Social Contract'.

refusal for the year 1978–9 and wages rose by around 10 per cent. With an unpopular wage control policy and over a million unemployed, Labour lost the 1979 general election.

The Conservative Government of Margaret Thatcher was determined to bring down inflation by limiting the amount of money the Government borrowed. By the time inflation started to fall in 1981, many firms had gone out of business and unemployment had risen to more than two million.

The Government was also determined to change the law on trade unions. The 1980 Employment Act forbade secondary picketing (picketing of people who were not on strike), and provided public money for secret ballots for trade union elections and before strikes. The 1984 Employment Act made it compulsory to have a secret ballot before a strike.

These changes brought the Government into conflict with the miners. On 12 March 1984 the miners went on a strike which was to last almost a year. The strike was over pit closures and although the Scottish and Yorkshire areas went on strike, Nottingham stayed at work. No ballot was called over the strike (the National Union of Miners was later fined £200 000 for running an illegal strike) and around 20 per cent of miners stayed at work.

The striking miners followed a policy of mass picketing which led to almost daily violence between police and pickets. This violence, along with the defiant speeches of the miners' leader, Arthur Scargill, lost the miners the sympathy of many middle class people. After 51 weeks the miners went back to work without any agreement. They had lost the strike. In 1985 there were 170 pits but by 1990 there were only 76.

The strike had shown how determined the Government was and this had an effect on the trade unions as the figures in Source 19.10 show.

## Source 19.10

| Year | Working days lost due to strikes |
|------|----------------------------------|
| 1979 | 29 474 000 |
| 1984 | 27 135 000 (22.4 million = miners' strike) |
| 1985 | 6 402 000 (4 million = miners) |
| 1986 | 1 920 000 |
| 1987 | 3 546 000 |
| 1997 | 235 000 |

| Year | Trade Union Membership |
|------|------------------------|
| 1976 | 12 400 000 |
| 1979 | 13 300 000 |
| 1986 | 10 500 000 |
| 1998 | 7 100 000 |

**CREDIT LEVEL**

## Activities

**1** What was the main reason for the General Strike of 1926? **(KU)**

**2** Compare the views on the General Strike in Sources 19.6 and 19.7. **(ENQ)**

**3** Use Sources 19.3, 19.4 and 19.5 and the account to explain the results of the strike. **(KU)**

**Role Play**

**4** Find out more about the causes of the General Strike and interview four people about their attitudes and reasons for being involved: a miner, a government minister, a coal owner, an OMS volunteer.

**5** a) After the Second World War, what three trade union activities often led to trouble with employers.

b) How did Esso try to end these practices?

**6** Draw and fill in the table below showing how the different parties dealt with the unions when they were in government.

| Year | Party | Action | Result |
|------|-------|--------|--------|
| 1967 | Lab. | Royal Commission | Govt give in |
| 1971 | | i.<br>ii.<br>iii. | |
| 1974 | Lab. | | |
| 1975–8 | | | |
| 1980 | | i.<br>ii.<br>iii. | |

# Glossary

**Artisans**
People working in trades and crafts.

**Asquith, Herbert**
Liberal, became Prime Minister in 1908 and supported many social reforms proposed by his Chancellor of the Exchequer, David Lloyd George, such as giving pensions to the elderly. But Asquith strongly opposed giving women the right to vote!

**Ballot**
System in which people vote by placing a mark beside the name of a candidate on an official piece of paper, in secret.

**Beeching, Dr**
Became responsible for running the railways in 1961. Produced two reports, in 1963 and 1965 claiming the railways were 'bloated' and inefficient. As a result 25% of lines were closed and 70 000 jobs lost. In 1967 railways were privatised again.

**Beveridge Report**
William Beveridge, a former civil servant, was appointed by the government of Winston Churchill to look into the problem of poverty in Britain. His report and recommendations on National Insurance became the basis for the Welfare State in Britain after 1945.

**Booth, Charles**
Son of a wealthy merchant family, he carried out a detailed survey of living conditions in the poorer parts of London.

**Cholera**
A disease which causes severe diarrhoea. It spreads quickly through infected water and symptoms develop very fast. Unless sufferers are treated quickly they become dehydrated and die.

**Churchill, Winston**
Began as a Conservative in 1900 but joined the Liberals in 1906. Rejoined the Conservatives in 1924 and became Prime Minister in 1940.

**Commission**
A group of people chosen by parliament to investigate a serious problem.

**Conscription**
This is when the government insists that men join the armed forces unless they are too old or have a good reason not to, such as poor health or a vital civilian job.

**Cottagers**
People who held small amounts of land and usually had to work for wealthier farmers/landowners.

**Craftsman**
Skilled workman who had learned his trade over years as an apprentice.

### Crofters
Owned/rented small pieces of land on which they grew some crops or had a few cattle, usually in the highlands and islands of Scotland.

### Davy safety lamp
A special lamp invented by a famous scientist, Sir Humphrey Davy, in 1815 for miners to use in pits where there was explosive gas (methane) and candles would have caused and explosion.

### Demarcation
In some industries, such as shipbuilding, certain jobs could only be done by certain workers. This could slow down production and result in loss of orders due to late delivery or high costs.

### Devolution
The process of passing control from the British parliament to governing bodies in Scotland and Wales.

### Enclosures
When open fields or strips of land were brought together by a wealthier farmer and enclosed by having barriers such as walls or hedges placed around them. Unpopular with many poorer people who lost land or income.

### Epidemic
This is when a disease spreads out of control, usually with fatal results for those who catch it.

### Free trade
Meant that goods could be imported into Britain without paying tariffs (tax) which often made them cheaper to buy but could cause problems for British businesses.

### Home Rule
The policy supported by Nationalist parties whereby countries such as Wales and Scotland would be run by their own elected governments and not by a British parliament.

### Liberals
By the start of the twentieth century there were three main political parties in Britain:

Liberals were supported by some of the wealthy, many in the middle class and some of the working class and were in favour of change

Conservatives represented mainly the landowners and wealthier people and were suspicious of change

Labour represented the working class and was only just emerging as a major party.

### Lloyd George, David
Liberal, strong supporter of social reforms, including votes for women after the First World War. He had been against war in 1914 but became leader of the coalition formed between Liberals and Conservatives in 1916 and led the war effort. He was elected Prime Minister in 1918 and passed an act giving many women the right to vote, as well as men over 21. By 1928 this was extended to include women over 21.

### Mass production
A way of making goods in factories which usually involved people working a shift on an assembly line, making or adding the same part to something like a car.

### Migration
Movement of people from one place to another in a country or from one country to another.

**Nationalisation**
The opposite process to privatisation, whereby services or industries are taken from private hands into government control – like railways in 1947.

**Pantry**
Storage cupboard.

**Prefab**
Single storey, prefabricated house, that is built in sections, manufactured after the Second World War to help overcome the shortage of homes caused by the bombing and the war.

**Privatisation**
The process of giving services or industries like transport or steel-making from government control into the hands of private companies, often leading to loss of jobs.

**Rural**
Country areas, away from towns.

**Slum**
Area of poverty and overcrowded, poor housing.

**Subsidies**
Money paid by the government to certain industries to help them survive.

**Suffrage**
Those included in the list of people able to vote.

**Suffragettes**
Those who tried to win the vote for women using various means, including violence such as destroying public property.

**Suffragists**
Those who used peaceful, non-violent means to try to win women the right to vote.

**Tariff**
Tax demanded by the government when goods are imported into Britain from abroad. Raised the price of such goods to the customer.

**Threshing**
Beating crops like wheat and oats to separate the grain from the rest of the plant.

**Trade depression**
This is when the sale of goods within countries and between countries slows down a lot and businesses have to close or lose workers.

**Tramcar**
Like a bus, except it was powered by electricity and ran on rails in the middle of the street.

**Wall Street Crash**
In 1929 many businesses in America ran in to difficulties and collapsed. People with shares in these companies lost lots of money and those who could rushed to sell their shares. Banks refused to give people back their money and there was widespread panic. Millions lost their jobs and their money.

# Internet resources

In the course of revising this series of books it became obvious that there is an extensive range of excellent resource materials freely and readily available on the internet for students and teachers alike. The range includes photographs and maps, video, text, simulations, sample questions and answers. In addition, there are sites offering help with the use of source extracts, other documents and different primary materials.

What follows is not offered as a complete or even comprehensive list of relevant sites but does represent valuable, interesting and enjoyable additional ways of learning about the past. Nor are the sites sorted by level. Several cover more than one context and these are listed first as general resources while others are under a more specific heading.

*No problems were encountered in using the sites in the list but, as with all internet sites, adverts and pop ups can turn up, sometimes because the site has used sponsors to pay for its place on the internet. The publisher and authors take no responsibility for the appearance of such unlooked-for intrusions. Please do type web addresses carefully and, if any unwelcome pop ups etc. do appear, close them immediately or they may be repeated or even freeze up your screen.*

## SITES COVERING SEVERAL CONTEXTS/TOPICS

www.bbc.co.uk/education/history
A very wide and easily accessible set of resources covering mainly British history, using video, photographs, documents, timelines, biographies and including the two World Wars. An easy site to find your way around.

http://www.bbc.co.uk/history/scottishhistory/
Well organised resources for ancient and modern Scotland and including links to film archives in a media museum.

www.spartacus.schoolnet.co.uk/
Offers very easily accessed resources for British, European and American history and encourages an on-line interactive approach with newsletters on learning and teaching History.

www.schoolshistory.org.uk
This site is produced by Laisterdyke H.S. Bradford and is designed to help students and teachers plan History revision on a number of British, European and other topics. The site also encourages teacher and student interaction and lists several other History sites and search engines for finding information. It is supported by the use of adverts.

www.schoolhistory.co.uk
Produced by Neale-Wade Community College, Cambridgeshire. Comprehensive range of (revision) resources, at different levels, on British, European and American topics, plus links to other relevant sites.

www.learninghistorysite.co.uk
British and European History at various levels, using text, photographs and some short videos.

www.learningcurve.pro.gov.uk
Public Record Office site for students and teachers, resources for British History such as documents, visuals and video and with links into a number of other useful History sites.

www.historygcse.org.
Well organised site, for teachers and students, with resources for European and American topics and numerous links to other sites and revision materials.

SPECIFIC SITES 1890 – 1945

www.firstworldwar.com
Very straightforward site providing documentary and visual materials in an easily accessible manner with no frills.

www.bbc.co.uk/history/war/wwone
Very comprehensive site including primary sources of many types, video, poetry, local information.

www.pro.gov.uk/pathways/firstworldwar
Public Record Office site on World War I, containing a wide range of documentary and photographic resources, well organised and accessible.

www.bbc.co.uk/history/war/wwtwo
Very comprehensive site on World War II, with written, photographic, video and audio resources and links to other sites and topics – such as propaganda, Hitler.

http://www.bbc.co.uk/schools/gcsebitesize/history/germany1919to45
Mainly intended for revision but with guidance on topics such as Germany 1919 – 1923, Weimar Germany, Hitler's rise to power, Hitler and Nazism, the Nazi state, source evaluation.

There are many, many other sites which can be accessed using a search engine like Google, to find topics as general as World War One, votes for women or as specific as the Somme or Emmeline Pankhurst. There are also valuable sites produced by schools, to make best use of research done by teachers and pupils. Two examples are given below.

http://www.ellonacademy.org.uk/
Follow the site map to the History department for resources and links to other sites.

www.passmores.essex.sch.uk/
Follow the site map to Humanities and then to History for resources and links to other sites.

# Index